STOPPING TO FEEL

ONE WOMAN'S JOURNEY TOWARD GENERATIONAL HEALING

S. L. COLLINS

Paperback ISBN: 979-8-9889757-8-6
Ebook ISBN: 979-8-9889757-9-3

To the daughters who love complicated fathers and to the mothers who are trying to break cycles.
And to Nadia and Natalie, for giving me grace in all my attempts.

AUTHOR'S NOTE

This book is a memoir and is based on my memories of certain events. I have done my best to recall them as accurately as possible, but the perceptions of others may differ from mine.

This book contains discussion of mature topics including alcoholism, child abuse, and eyewitness accounts of death.

A LETTER TO MY FATHER

Dear Dad:

If everyone knew the truth about the things you did over the years, would they still sing your praises? Would they still say that you were "a hero" and an "upstanding citizen" and "one of the good guys"? I have held your secrets for so long that at some point they began to feel like my own. They burned my insides, struggling to stay buried and simultaneously yearning to break free. Did I hide these secrets for you, or for me?

I never wanted to tell the whole truth to anybody, because I didn't want them to judge you. I could always forgive you, but what if they could not? What then? Did keeping your secrets keep you safe, or did it keep me safe? Maybe I kept your secrets for me, because if I revealed them, I'd have to be honest with myself and realize how incredibly selfish you could be, and sometimes that truth was too painful for me to bear.

Now you are gone, and I feel ready to share my story. But how can I tell my truth without revealing some of yours? Who I am is so intertwined with who you are—were—that I must unlock the secrets. We are so similar, and yet, so very different. And despite it all—no, perhaps, because of it all—I love you more than ever.

*You taught me to put on a tough face, push through adversity and keep moving. After all, if you just keep moving, you won't crash. But I was never as good at running as you were, Dad. I could only move for so long. I needed to stop, to stand still. And you know what? When I stopped, the feelings flooded me and I **did** crash. But it's okay. I am okay. Sometimes, we need the crash because there's beauty in the breakdown.*

You wanted to leave a legacy of generational wealth and prosperity, but you left me so much more. Your legacy is one of forgiveness and freedom from pain. We are only as sick as our secrets, Dad, and we are no longer sick. You struggled in silence for so long. Let me help set you free, by releasing us one secret at a time. Because if there's one thing you taught me in this life, it is that everyone deserves love—no matter their secrets.

-Sasha Boom

PROLOGUE: WHO HE WAS

There was nobody else in the entire world like my dad. It sounds cliché, but it's true. Whenever I try to explain him, I come up short. I feel like I don't have enough words to describe him in a way that will do him justice. He was simultaneously the simplest and the most complex man that I have ever known.

Dad was a tall and lean 6' 3". He exercised almost every day of his life: running, hiking, biking, climbing, and weightlifting. He once wrote that his ideal perfect day was one filled with exercise—traveling across two counties and mountain ranges, just for the pleasure of hiking and climbing a specific set of stairs. Although he exercised and lifted weights daily, he didn't ever get bulky or grossly muscular, like those weightlifters who grunt excessively at the gym, their veins popping out of their overly swollen biceps. No, Dad preferred to keep a low profile, and his calves certainly never gave him away. No matter how much he exercised, he never seemed capable of building calf muscles. His legs remained stick straight and narrow.

He was a solitary man—he didn't like big crowds and he didn't need people around him. But at the same time, he constantly built connections everywhere he went. There were no strangers to him.

He was never too embarrassed or proud to make friends with random people. The man from Europe he met while hiking the Pacific Crest Trail in 1983, became a lifelong friend and pen-pal. The man who sold him his car in 2003 ended up living with him for a few months in 2009. The woman who sat next to him on the flight to New Zealand in 2014 kept in touch with him for the rest of his life. He knew all my friends in high school. Not because I had introduced them to him, but because he did his own reconnaissance missions to find out more about them. He was a connector.

Most of the time, when I told people my dad's name, they'd say, "Oh, I know him!" Yet whenever I heard that people knew Dad, I instantly felt nervous. *How* did they know him and *which* Dad did they know? Dad had so many sides to him, I never knew which one he presented to various people. Did they know him from the gym? The coffee shops? Parole? If it was a woman, did he save her from some toxic ex-boyfriend or did he try to date her? Did they see him happy or angry? Breaking rules or following them?

His voice was so loud—it carried for hundreds of yards. Dad was completely incapable of whispering. Ironic, given how many secrets he kept.

I dreaded going to the movie theatre with him, because he would attempt to have conversations at normal volume, not caring whether he was interrupting all the other movie-goers. Speaking of movies—he could never sit still in them. When we'd try to watch a movie at home, he would always get up and offer us things multiple times—"Popcorn? Water? Another pillow? Another blanket? Footrest?" I can't think of one single movie that we watched from start to finish together without interruption.

Dad never complained about anything, least of all food. He once told me that he didn't need recipes because he'd just eat the ingredients. I have vivid memories of him eating sandwiches in the kitchen of our childhood home. Two pieces of San Luis Sourdough, with a pound of deli turkey in the middle, held together by a copious amount of mayonnaise—the gelatinous goo seeping through the holes of the sourdough. Mom, with her arms crossed in the corner of the kitchen, annoyed that, once again, he had eaten all the week's deli meat in one sitting.

In recent years, his meal of choice was El Pollo Loco. The eight-piece family meal was his favorite thing to randomly drop by our house. Every single time he'd bring it, he would comment on how good it was, and how much food was included in the family meal deal. If anybody had leftovers, he'd add their food to his own plate and douse it with the remaining Pico de Gallo. He left nothing uneaten—he didn't believe in waste.

He rarely ever ate junk food—occasionally, he would indulge in a regular Coke or a Snickers bar, and then he'd tell us about it for months. "I had my first Snickers bar in almost three years!" As if that were a badge of honor. As if he couldn't just enjoy a Snickers whenever he wanted.

Dad also *loved* to tell people what to do. He was full of grand ideas for what people could do to make their lives better. People's lives would improve if they just did what he said. After all, he knew best. At least, that's what he thought. These ideas came from a place of love, but he also didn't take kindly to people who didn't follow his instructions. He certainly never stopped to consider whether people actually *wanted* his advice. One time, my sister offhandedly mentioned an interest in Eastern medicine. For the next five years, he would give her flyers for acupuncture schools and clinics every time he saw her. Eventually, his pestering became so persistent that she lost all interest in pursuing it altogether.

Dad rarely told people where he was going or what he was doing. He thrived on the element of surprise. He liked to stay one step ahead of everyone. As a result, he would frequently show up at places completely unexpectedly. More than once, he would show up at my work without warning, just to check in on me. I was so embarrassed by his random appearing acts that when I got a new job in my early twenties, I didn't tell him about it for almost a year. I didn't want him showing up unannounced and embarrassing me in front of my new coworkers.

The Dad I loved was adventurous, fun-loving, and generous. This version of Dad believed that all a person needed to have a good adventure was a good attitude, a bathing suit, and tennis shoes. Thanks to Dad, I never go on a trip without packing a bathing suit. This version of Dad caught lizards barehanded and jumped rope on rotting tree stumps on the side of the road. He said, "Whoa Nelly" and laughed at his own stories before the punchline, because he knew what was coming next. This version of Dad rubbed aloe vera on skinned knees and took nine of my friends to Hurricane Harbor water park for my eighth birthday. He taught himself how to draw cartoons on a whiteboard in our garage and taught us how to hold our breath in freezing cold creek water before running to a hot jacuzzi, just like our Finnish ancestors. He was a practical joker. He loved good-natured fun. He was the dad of my childhood. The strong, brave, fun, and fearless Dad.

But somewhere along the way, I met another version of my dad. This version of Dad was loud, stubborn, and angry. He spoke with authority, and you didn't dare talk back. He was no longer boyish and fun, but cold and uninviting. This version of Dad frightened and confused me. This Dad didn't teach lessons, he shut down questions. This version of Dad talked over you, refused to listen to you and directed all conversations. This Dad insisted that it was his way or the highway. This version was self-righteous and quick to anger. He made rash decisions and held grudges.

I only wanted people to know the good sides of Dad, because I was proud of that Dad. I loved that Dad. I didn't want people to know his troubled side. When I met people who knew Dad, I held my breath and hoped they didn't know *this* version of Dad. The version I tried to keep secret.

Telling the story of my relationship with my dad is a constant internal battle. I want to tell everyone the truth about everything, to have no more secrets, and to be free. But at the same time, I want to protect him and the image he so perfectly crafted for his entire life. I am afraid that if I tell the whole truth about him, people will no longer like him. How silly is that? Why am I worried about the reputation of a dead man? I know I loved him, and that should be all that matters. But it's not. I feel like I want to guard his truth, but at what cost?

The truth is, my dad was a good man who helped a lot of people in his life. But the truth is seldom so simple. The truth is, he was a good man, who *also* made a lot of terrible decisions, and those decisions left a lot collateral damage in his wake.

His stories deserve to be told, but so do mine.

This is mine.

PART I

1

GO TIME: JULY 27, 2024

"Sasha, I think it's 'Go-Time.'" Dad's voice cracked over the phone as I bent over toward the garage fridge, balancing the phone between my ear and my shoulder.

I straightened up. The hair on my forearms stood on end as he continued, "I know we were supposed to have a family talk with your sister on Saturday, but I cannot wait that long. I have been in bed for three days. It's bad. I need to get back to California *now*."

It had only been three days since his last CAT scan, the results of which were horrific. *Extensive metastasis. Multiple lesions—lung, liver, peritoneal. Persistent left adrenal lesions.* All of these growths while on chemotherapy.

When he'd received the test results three days before—Tuesday night—he couldn't bring himself to call me. I knew he had the scan in the morning and that the results must have been bad, because he didn't send me the results right away. His friend Gary, whom I had dubbed "the Mole" for his constant funneling of information to me, had called me around 6 p.m. that day. I had been putting the kids to bed and hadn't been able to talk. But I knew. If Dad was radio silent, and Gary was calling, it was bad.

A few hours later, Dad finally texted me:

Well now. Not good news. Widespread and spreading. I have not spoken with Dr. Lambert, but my guess is that my chemo days are over. Maybe God will decide to save me, by some form of a miracle healing. If not, the big guy may be getting ready for my next big adventure! Please forward this to Launa. Nobody else yet. I need time to think. No worries. Love Dad.

"No worries." As if he hadn't just texted me the news that the end of his life was near.

Dad was never one for emotional discussions—straight to the point, no bullshit. So, over the years, I had adopted the same style of communication with him. It made it easier to handle his blasé approach if I approached it the same way. In the past, when I tried to send more emotional messages via text, he would respond with a sunglasses emoji—"Cool." It was not cool. But it was Dad.

When shit hit the fan, Dad tended to make rash decisions. A few hours after texting me his scan results, he started texting me about his house. *The* house. "Basecamp Blaine." A house we told him not to buy, but of course he did anyway.

I am thinking of listing my place in a few days. List at about 600 thousand. I might net 200 plus? I think I should do it. Your position? Not done fighting! Reset time!

Then, a few minutes later:

My place would make an awesome west coast family retreat. Generational wealth. Your kids might live here! I've done all the hard work. It's easy now and the 1ˢᵗ mortgage is at a fixed 3.5%!

In that moment, my sole job was to convince him not to sell the property. Ironic, since I had spent a lot of time in 2021 trying to convince him not to buy the property in the first place. But at that point, we could not afford for him to sell it—literally and figuratively. If he sold it, lord only knew what he would do next.

I knew he was overwhelmed, so I told him to take a few days to think. We could have a family discussion on Saturday to decide what to do about the house, his health, his future, and everything in between.

But that discussion never came because here he was, on Thursday night, panicking.

"I need to get to California as soon as possible—I cannot wait until Saturday to talk. By Saturday, I should be in California."

I was trying—and failing—to take in this new information and process it.

"Where are you going to go in California?" I asked.

"Your house!" he answered without missing a beat.

It was never the plan for Dad to be at my house when he was dying. It wasn't his plan, and it wasn't my plan. When he moved to Washington, he always said that when it came time for him to need hospice, he would come back to California and go a friend's house in Simi Valley for "a few months" and then when hospice was needed, he would go to Serenity House or Serra House in Santa Barbara to live out his final days.

And yet, here he was saying that he was coming to my house. I should have been mad, but instead, I was glad. Glad that he trusted me enough to come here, even if temporarily. I never understood why he would want to go to his friend's house first—it was hot as hell in Simi Valley and he had plenty of other family members to help.

Dad continued, "I haven't been able to get out of bed in three days. The pain is intense."

I told him we would get him on a flight to California right away. But he insisted that he would drive. He wanted his car in California, and he wouldn't be leaving it in Washington.

"Dad, you just told me you haven't been out of bed in three days —how are you going to drive yourself to California?"

Of course, as usual, Dad had a plan.

"I am going to leave tomorrow morning. I will get up early and 'Bonzi it' eight hours to Herman's house in Grants Pass, Oregon. I will spend the night and rest there. Then I will get up on Saturday and 'Bonzi it' to Ted's house in Northern California. I will spend the night and then I will 'Bonzi it' to your house in Ventura and be there by Sunday."

He was totally serious. The man was dying of cancer, had not gotten out of bed in three days, and yet he was planning a solo two-state road trip back to California. As insane as it sounded, I knew he could do it. Dad was the master of "mind over matter"—if he wanted to do it, he did it. He would have done it, but I would not let him. Not this time.

I immediately called my sister Launa and told her what was going on. Our mom was in San Diego visiting, so Launa put it on speaker. We worked through various options—could we buy him a plane ticket? Could we fly up one of our spouses to drive him down? Could his roommate Marty drive him down?

In the end, we decided to fly up and get him ourselves. We wouldn't ask him—we'd tell him. Together, the two of us booked tickets. Then, I called Dad and told him, "We are coming to get you." Dad never asked for help, and especially not from the two of us. But, in that moment, he accepted it.

"Okay," he said. "I'm really pleased you are coming. It will be a great adventure."

Launa and I prepared for one last Bonzi trip with Dad.

2

CHILDHOOD ADVENTURES

M y childhood with Dad was full of adventures. There were no limits to what he thought my younger sister and I could do. We rode bikes, climbed trees, played sports, and hiked mountains.

Summers were spent with my dad taking us on adventures to Zuma beach. We would head down PCH, stop at Trancas Market and load up on snacks. Back then, the market was not a fancy organic market, teeming with hipsters. No, Trancas Market was just that—a market. A plain old grocery store that we could afford. We spent all day at the beach, playing in the sand, freckles emerging on our noses.

What I loved most about those beach days with Dad was that he was always engaged with us. He wasn't the kind of Dad who would sit on the beach under an umbrella with a beer in hand. Dad enjoyed the beach with us—on the shore, he used his strong arms to help us build sandcastles and moats. He walked with us down the beach while we collected sand crabs and looked for shells. When we ventured out into the water, he came too. He was the first to jump in and dive under the waves. He put us atop boogie boards and pulled us out into the ocean, always pushing the limits on how deep we could go. He stood with us while the waves rolled in, holding onto the back of our boogie board, poised and ready to push us into the waves.

Most of these beach adventures were with Dad only. At the time, I thought it was because he was the fun parent. Now, as a mother myself, I realize it was because my mom was likely at home doing all the things involved with keeping our household running. Groceries. Laundry. School shopping. That, or she just preferred the calmness of a quiet house without kids for one afternoon.

One summer when I was a young girl, Dad hosted some friends from Australia. To this day, I don't know how they were related to my dad—distant cousins, perhaps? Our family called them "the Aussies"—Matt, Allison, and one other friend whose name I cannot remember. They rolled up to our house one day in a beat-up utility van—matte gray, with rusted wheels and graffiti on the side. It looked like the kind of van that Dad would normally tell us to be wary of and not walk too close to the sliding door, lest a stranger reach out and grab us.

But this van wasn't to be feared, this van was revered by Dad as a vessel for adventure. Immediately, Dad told us that we were going on an adventure to hike some local creeks with our new Aussie friends. Even at a young age, I knew the drill. An adventure with Dad required only four things: shorts, a T-shirt, a bathing suit, and a good attitude. Wimp-a-saruses need not apply.

My sister and I gathered up our usual gear and headed to the van to load up. We opened the door and, much to our surprise, there were no seats inside. The entire back of the van was empty—a shell of a vehicle. The only thing inside was the driver's seat, the passenger seat, and fifteen feet of hollow, empty space.

Not to be deterred, Dad grabbed a dolly, hefted a spare couch from our garage onto it and loaded the couch into the back of the van. He then proceeded to give us bike helmets and grabbed a piece of rope from the garage. He sat us on the couch, fastened our bike helmets on, and strapped us to the couch with the rope as a makeshift seatbelt. We thought this was the most hilarious thing we had ever seen. I don't know where my mom was that day, but I have a feeling she would not have found it quite as hilarious. This was the 1990s after all—not the 1970s. We knew better!

The adventure with the Aussies in the couch van was one of my favorite memories from childhood. It was a day marked with adventure, elation, and security. The fact that the van didn't have seats, let alone seatbelts, didn't stop my dad from allowing us to have a great time exploring. He made me feel safe and cared for when he strapped me onto that couch with the bike helmet and rope. He drove as slowly as possible to ensure the couch didn't fly around the back of the van too much, and when we got to our destination, the creek, he let us run wild and free.

ANOTHER TIME, Dad had the great idea to go to for a bike ride. In true Dad fashion, this was not just any bike ride, it was a great adventure. He and Mom loaded up our van full of friends and bikes and drove us twenty-five miles to the Santa Monica Mountains.

The Santa Monica Mountains stretch forty miles along the Southern California coast, separating the Conejo Valley from the Pacific Ocean. The trail where Dad took us to starts at the top of Newbury Park and winds down through the Boney Mountain trail, landing at Thornhill Broom at the bottom of the mountain.

Many experienced mountain bikers ride through the canyon and avid hikers dot the trails. Among all the adult hikers and mountain bikers was Dad and a gang of wily children—some of whom were still using training wheels. To this day, we may still be the only group of six- and eight-year-olds who went on a trek down that mountain and through the canyon.

Mom dropped us off at the trailhead and drove down to wait for us at the beach at the bottom. Dad gave the kids a pep talk about sticking together and avoiding poison ivy, and then we were off.

Gang of kids near the bottom of Sycamore Canyon.

Though the scenery was beautiful, I remember being terrified in the beginning. The road is not meant for bikes with training wheels and rainbow streamers. The descent to the beach is not gradual. The trail starts off on a steep and winding concrete road, which caused my bike to pick up speed faster than I was comfortable with. Dad was ten yards ahead of me when I cried out in fear, "Dad!! I am going too fast!"

Dad turned and hollered, "Hold on tight and just keep pedaling!" As he jogged ahead to the younger kids in front, he turned his head back again and yelled over his shoulder, "Most importantly, don't fall off your bike or you will knock out your teeth and get blood all over the trail!" He said this with a glint in his eye as a smile spread across his cheeks. He was always trying to turn fear into humor and tears into laughter.

I held on for dear life and kept pedaling—Dad was right, if I just kept moving, I wouldn't crash.

APTLY NAMED, Foothill Road runs along the base of the foothills in Ventura, connecting the sunny East Side of town with the breezy and foggy West Side. Nestled halfway between the two edges of the city lies Arroyo Verde Park, a quiet sanctuary tucked into the mountains, flanked on either side by rows of houses.

An easy hiking path winds along the edges of the horseshoe-shaped park, allowing hikers of all ages and strength levels to enjoy the beauty. In spring, mustard flowers line the edges of the path, their yellow faces stretching up toward the sun. The *crack* of baseballs being flung into the air reverberates throughout the canyon, as children rounded bases in baseball fields tucked back into the corner of the park.

Almost every family we knew hiked at Arroyo Verde. It was an easy spot for parents to allow their kids to run along the trails, to tire them out before bedtime. Halfway through the park, the trail slopes down toward a simple playground, where children laugh as they chase their friends through the sand. The playground was the place where normal families hung out.

Dad didn't want us to be normal though, he wanted us to be extraordinary—to do things differently, to push harder and see more.

While other families stopped at the playground, or continued along the well-marked circular loop, Dad took us to the back of the park. Off to the side of the marked trail, a small path cut up the side of the mountain. Hardly any hikers used this path as evidenced by how much narrower it was than the marked trail—roughly a quarter of the size.

The path went straight up the side of the mountain, leaving the hiker completely exposed to the sun. There were no winding corners, no shaded spots to rest. At some point, the trail was too steep for our young bodies, and we resorted to crawling on all fours, pretending to be wild animals, traversing the mountains in search of water. The sun beat down on our faces and the dust from the lesser traveled path clung to our legs, covering us in a layer of filth.

As with most of our hikes with Dad—we whined and we cried, but we kept going.

When we got to the top, we knew why he had pushed us.

Those who stayed on the trail saw the park. Those who dared to climb up the path saw the world—the entire county stretched before us, and the ocean twinkled in the distance. Behind us stood the Topa Topa mountain range. The clear blue sky was punctured by the tips of mountains we never knew existed until that moment.

We took in the view for a short period of time before Dad wanted to go back—he didn't ever sit for long. But our legs were tired, and we were not able to go any further, even if it was downhill.

Dad hoisted us both onto his body like a human pack mule. Launa got up first. She climbed up his back and sat atop his broad shoulders, her stomach nestled against the back of his head. I was taller and heavier, so I climbed on Dad's back. My spindly legs wrapped around his midsection; my arms wrapped tightly around his neck.

"Hang on tight!" he said with a boyish chuckle. And then he started to run.

We picked up speed quickly as he ran straight down the side of the mountain. Dust flew everywhere. The wind whipped my face and my hair billowed behind me. "Whoaaaa Nelly!" Dad yelled, as he jumped over a jagged rock. We squealed with delight as our father carried us down the mountain, none of us ever stopping to think of what would happen to us if he stumbled and fell.

My CHILDHOOD WAS full of days like this. Bike days. Beach days. Creek days. Adventure days. Hiking Days. By all accounts, it was an incredibly happy childhood. I felt loved and supported by both of my parents. But beneath that happiness was an anxiety—an uncertainty that has taken me three decades to peel back and dissect. Because even as a young child, underneath the laughter and adventure, I intuitively felt the undercurrent of something a little less sturdy.

Before riding down Sycamore Canyon.

3

SHAMBALA

O ur white Jeep Cherokee shook violently as Dad navigated it up the steep hills and through the deep potholes that littered the dirt road before us.

I peered through my window in the back seat. Although it was dusted with red dirt, I could still make out the metal cages stacked high underneath the shabby wooden outpost, large wild cats squished inside of them.

Behind a large chain-link fence, a panther paced anxiously. A lion's roar filled the air at the same time Dad hit the creek. Water splashed up, creating rivulets through the dirt-crusted windows.

We crested the top of the hill, and I turned to peek at the elephants—my favorite part of this drive. Their trunks dipped into murky water, and they let out a large *pfffffffft* to rival the roar of the lion.

Though I didn't realize it at the time, I later learned that my grandparents lived behind Shambala Preserve, a desert sanctuary established by the actress Tippi Hedren. The preserve included dozens of large cats, elephants, and other wild animals that had been retired from movie sets, circuses, and zoos.

I lost sight of the panthers and elephants as Dad guided the Jeep over the railroad tracks and toward my grandparents' mobile home.

The air conditioning in our Jeep did nothing to beat back the temperature of Soledad Canyon, and I could feel the sticky heat of the day before we even got out of the car.

The crunch of the tires rolling over the gravel announced our arrival, and I saw my grandfather emerge from the single-wide mobile home. He was short and stocky. A brown polo shirt stretched slightly across the soft pooch of his stomach and an off-white captain's hat sat atop his head. A small black dog ran through his legs and toward our car.

"Sputnik, *nyet!*" he barked curtly at the dog in his thick Russian accent.

My grandfather turned to look at us getting out of the car. There was no hint of a smile on his face. No indication that he was happy to see his son or granddaughters.

"Heyyyyy, Papa," Dad said in a reserved voice, exposing an uncharacteristic deference to this short and stoic man.

If the heat outside was sticky, inside the trailer was stifling. The windows were closed tightly, and a weak breeze wafted toward us from a small table fan. The entire room smelled of a nauseous combination of sweat and dirt.

My sister and I sat on a firm floral couch with our hands clasped tightly together and shoved between our knees. We didn't dare speak.

Opposite us, our grandmother sat on a couch, separated from us by a small oval-shaped coffee table. Her button-up blouse was half-a-size too small, and her large chest appeared to be pressing against it, threatening to break off the buttons. A drab brown skirt fell almost onto her loosely crossed ankles.

She motioned toward the coffee table, where she had placed a small candy bowl, filled with strawberry-shaped candies. I could feel the crinkle of the metallic wrapper in my small hands even before she handed me one.

On the other side of the living room was a metal kitchen sink and a small refrigerator. My grandfather muttered unintelligibly as he walked through what I presumed was a kitchen, although I don't remember seeing any actual food anywhere. Was there even a kitchen table? I don't recall.

Though I had been here before, this place was still unfamiliar to me, as were my grandparents. Their trailer was a place we rarely frequented, even though it was less than an hour's drive from our house. My dad would drive further than that to take us to a good beach. Why did we rarely come here?

Me as a kid in front of a danger sign.

I have very few memories from inside that trailer. Most likely because, almost as soon as we came in, my sister and I were ushered back outside so the grownups could talk.

Aside from the out-of-place jungle animals we passed on our way in, there was no sign of life in that dusty and drab canyon. In front of the trailer, a circle of miniature cacti created the outline of a tether-ball court. The clink of the metal chain hitting the pole echoed off the sides of the canyon. Twenty feet to the right, the ground was littered with broken clay pucks. A makeshift skeet-shooting machine pointed to the side of a hill.

I dragged my toes through the dirt and stared at a small wooden shack in the distance.

The bang of the metal screen door brought my focus back to the trailer. My dad stood tall with his muscular arms flexing beneath his white T-shirt. My grandfather followed behind him. Though his face was full of wrinkles and sunspots, his stomach was pooched in the middle, and he was a full head shorter than my dad, my grandfather was the more intimidating figure.

"Time to go, girls," Dad grunted. He loaded us into the Jeep to make the trek back through the canyon, over the railroad tracks, past the elephants and panthers and to the freeway below.

THOUGH I HAD no real emotional connection to my grandfather and grandmother, I felt connected to my dad's side of the family through the stories that he shared with us about my grandparents and how they came to America. My grandparents didn't always live in that strange desolate canyon in a single-wide trailer—they lived whole lifetimes before they arrived there.

From a young age, my dad would share with me stories of my Russian and Finnish heritage. The story, as I was told, was this:

Supposedly, my grandfather was born in Russia. He was one of five or six children—my dad was never certain of the actual number. My great-grandparents were taken to the gulags when my grandfather was a young boy, and according to family lore, my grandfather and his siblings became orphans and started living on the streets.

Eventually, my grandfather became a captain in the Red Army of the Soviet Union. How he went from abandoned orphan to captain in an army is anyone's guess. At some point, he defected from the Red Army and went into hiding but was later caught by the Finnish army. Somehow, between defecting from one army and being caught by another, he was taken in by wealthy landowners who had extra space in their barn. My grandfather hid in the barn for weeks, if not months. Eventually, he fell in love with the daughter of a nearby landowner. Just a few short weeks after they met, they married. I learned many years later that at the time of their marriage, my grandfather was nearly thirty and my grandmother was only eighteen.

Shortly after their marriage, in the late 1940s, my grandparents began their journey to immigrate to America. They country-hopped from Finland to Sweden to Ireland, until they eventually boarded a boat for America. Along the way, my grandmother gave birth to my four eldest uncles.

My grandfather and the two oldest sons arrived in New York in 1952. My grandmother stayed behind in Ireland with the youngest two until she was able to build up strength for the journey.

After a short stay in New York, the family ended up in the San Fernando Valley in Southern California, where my grandfather became a taxi driver, and my grandmother continued to have children—one after another for the next fifteen years. My grandmother's last pregnancy was twins—but the eleventh child, a girl, died in childbirth. My father was the middle child of the bunch.

Though my grandmother was born to a wealthy Finnish family, they disowned her when she married my grandfather, a Russian. In America, she and my grandfather were forced to make it on their own. To build their own life. To live the American Dream.

And I was made to believe that they made it—they achieved the

American Dream by living and raising their children in Southern California. Sure, times were tough having ten children, but they had done it. In my mind, my father was proof of their achievements.

I remember learning that my grandfather had written a book about his experiences in the Red Army, going into hiding in Finland and eventually meeting my grandmother. I have distinct memories of my father showing me drafts of my grandfather's manuscript. Approximately 200 pages of waxy paper held a mysterious story. The manuscript was held together by a clipboard. Dad would sometimes sit in front of the fireplace in our house, wearing his long robe, legs crossed with the clipboard balanced atop his bent knee. He would flip through the pages while sipping a glass of wine.

I wondered when I would be old enough to read the whole story.

4

YOUNG WOUNDS

Our grey-and-white house stood on the corner of a well-trafficked intersection just four blocks from our elementary school. A friend from down the road walked to school with her mom and their dog every day. One day, they offered to pick me up on their way so I could walk with them. I was so excited! I dressed in my new Eddie Bauer pantsuit—silky white pants adorned with purple flowers, with a matching vest worn over a purple shirt. A large purple scrunchie held back my straight, sun-kissed hair.

I waited for them to crest the short hill from their house to mine, expecting to see their golden retriever at any moment. But the minutes ticked by, and they had not yet appeared. I started to grow worried—what if they never came? What if I missed the bell? What if I was late?

"I need to go to school," I stammered. "I'm going to be late!"

It was just me and Dad there that day—an abnormal morning since he was normally gone before the sun came up. I don't remember where my mom and sister were.

Not knowing what time school started and relying on the time-telling of a six-year-old, Dad agreed. "Okay, well, good thing you have your tennis shoes on—run, grasshopper!"

With that, I threw on my purple Jansport backpack and took off toward school. I ran, alone, like my life depended on it. The normally full sidewalk was devoid of other children—a sure sign that I was, in fact, late. I was crossing Drexel Avenue by myself when I lost my footing. My backpack flipped over my head and carried me down with it. The granular asphalt stuck in the palms of my hands, and I looked in horror as blood seeped through my white pantsuit, my damaged knee protruding from the newly formed rip.

I gathered myself and limped back home, blood trickling down my legs.

At home I found Catherine and her mom at my front door, confused about why I was limping up the street covered in blood, rather than waiting for them on my porch like we had planned. It didn't occur to me until much later that the reason the sidewalks weren't filled with other children walking to school wasn't because I was late—but because I couldn't tell time, and I was twenty minutes early.

Dad took one look at me and said, "Whoa Nelly, looks like you took a good spill! Let's wash up that leg and get you some aloe vera."

He sat me on the counter and cleaned out my knee with precision—he flushed it with water and was careful to get all the gravel and asphalt pieces out. He broke off a piece of fresh aloe vera from the yard and smeared the cool gel onto the wound. He topped it off with a band aid and a grin—"I guess the street won this one, huh?"

My knee was fixed, but my pride was wounded, and my anxiety remained. I was so grateful to have a dad who could fix up the physical wounds, but I wouldn't realize for two more decades how bad he was at acknowledging and healing emotional ones.

In the early 1990s, Polly Pockets were all the rage. Teeny tiny dolls that fit inside of compact little houses with pieces that got lost almost instantly upon opening the packages. My friends and I were lucky enough to have received some for our birthdays one year, and they were all we played with for a while. But suddenly, that changed.

In October 1993, my dad's brother Paul died. I was six years old and in the first grade. To be honest, until I learned that he had died, I didn't even know my dad *had* a brother named Paul. As a child, my dad's family was always a mystery to me—I found them and their dusty trailer in the canyon a bit frightening. Their English was poor, and they smelled stale. We only visited them a handful of times and I only have one or two memories of them ever coming to our house in Ventura.

I don't remember how I even found out that this mystery uncle had died. I don't think my parents discussed it with me, so I likely just overheard them talking about it.

I didn't really understand what dying was—I just knew it was bad and I got a sense that I should be sad about it.

So, as I walked home from school with my friend one day in October, I boldly proclaimed that we could no longer call Polly Pocket by her real name "Polly"—it was too close to the name of my uncle Paul, and he was dead. Dead was bad, and we couldn't play with dead people names, and so Polly (or Pauly?) Pocket would have to be renamed.

She was confused. "Who is Uncle Paul? I didn't know you had an Uncle Paul?"

"Well, I did, and he died, so we cannot say his name anymore because it is sad for my dad," I stated indignantly.

I never talked about this with anybody except her. I don't remember ever talking about it with my mom or my dad. Perhaps we didn't discuss it because they felt I was too young, or that I wouldn't care, because I didn't even know I had an Uncle Paul to begin with.

It's true, I didn't know Paul, and so I couldn't be sad about his passing. But there was still a feeling of uncertainty—of knowing that something bad had happened, but having no real context for how it fit into my life.

And so, I shoved that confusion and uncertainty into a tight ball and tucked it away. I snapped the door shut and slipped those feelings into my back pocket, just like those tiny plastic Polly Pocket houses.

NOT LONG AFTER PAUL DIED, my dad's mom—my grandmother—got sick. I know now that she had cancer, but I didn't know it then. All I knew was that one day she was in that dusty old trailer and the next she was in a hospital.

Mom and I visited the hospital where she had been admitted. I remember peeking in her room and seeing her legs on top of the hospital bed, but I could not take another step forward. Instead, I stayed in the hallway and refused to go inside her room. If I close my eyes, I can still see the long hallway—the lack of decorations and the silence made it cold and uninviting. While my mother visited with my grandma, I stared down at the seafoam-green tile outside my grandmother's hospital room, where I crouched down and waited for my mom to emerge.

My mom and I visited the hospital alone. My sister was too young and stayed home with a babysitter. My dad was on a trip to Finland. He had gone back to find my grandmother's family and to visit the family farm—the one she left behind when she married my grandfather. Dad's visit to Finland was a pilgrimage of sorts, meant to be a chance to see where he had come from and to learn more about his family still there. But Dad's trip was cut short by my grandmother's untimely death. Almost immediately after he arrived in Finland, he turned around and flew home.

A week later, my parents dressed in formal black clothing and loaded my sister and me into our Jeep. The next memory I have is of arriving at our friend's house. A two-story house perched at the top of a cul-de-sac. I was mesmerized by the gorgeous harp that sat on display inside of the bay window in front of the house. Sun splashed off its marvelous gold curves.

My parents were going to my grandmother's funeral. My sister and I were going to a playdate. No need to bother us with all that sadness.

5

BACKPACKS AND BLOODY NOSES

It was a Thursday evening in April. The air was crisp and warm, a nearby power line gently buzzing in the background. Dirt covered my pants and one small bead of sweat lingered in my hairline—thick enough to feel, but not heavy enough to fall. It was the end of a long softball game, and we were so close to finishing. We just needed to strike out one more batter. My friend was on the mound—tired, but determined to close it out. I squatted behind home plate, the catcher's gear squeaking with every move I made.

Mom was in the dugout, organizing the bat bags before the inning ended. Dad stood in the entryway of the dugout, leaning against the pole, cheering for us. "Okay, Sasha Boom—here we go, one more batter!"

The pitcher wound up, bit her lip, and threw a pitch as hard as she could. The bat connected—a line drive straight to second base. She caught it, and victory was ours!

We cheered with pride. Nobody was prouder of us than Dad in the dugout.

"You girls kicked ass!" a parent shouted from the bleachers.

"Hey now, we don't talk like that here," Dad said sternly, before turning to us. "Girls—you opened a can of whoop-i-lation on that team!"

After the game, we gathered in the alley behind the softball field. The neon sign from the laundromat flicked on as the sun began to set.

"Pleasseeeeeee, can we go get pizza, please?!" we begged.

"Okay, fine, we can go to Santino's!" Mom relented, after glancing sideways at the other moms to confirm.

"YES!" we cheered, as we began to run down the alley toward the aged and musty pizza place that had become a weekly staple in our diets. The sound of our plastic cleats striking the asphalt echoed throughout the alley. *Click clack, click clack, click clack.*

Inside Santino's was dark and dank. The booths were made up of cracking old red vinyl—the kind that assured you stayed put until you were done eating, because your legs would inevitably sweat and stick to the seat.

Grease pooled on top of the pizza, shimmering slightly under the dim light. As the beer foam inched closer to the bottom of each plastic pitcher, our parents' laughs grew louder and their voices more boisterous. More and more coins spilled from their wallets, as they encouraged us to play another round of Pac Man in the arcade room while they ordered another round.

Somewhere between the sticky red vinyl and the cramped arcade room, a feeling started to grow inside of me. We were supposed to be having fun and celebrating our victory, and yet that threatening feeling began to rise inside of my throat.

Wham! Wham! The pixelated figured on the Mortal Kombat arcade screen leapt up and landed a kick against an opponent's chest. I felt as if I had been struck myself. My chest was tight, my breath came short. I felt outside of my body as I quickly made up an excuse to leave the arcade room and go back to the parents' table.

"Mom, we need to go home right now," I whispered in her ear.

"What? How come? We just got here!" Her head was turned halfway toward me, while she tried to catch the punchline of another grown-up's story.

"My homework is due tomorrow, and I need to make sure it is in my backpack," I mumbled.

"Oh, don't worry, I put it in there before the game," Mom responded nonchalantly. "Go back and play." And she turned back to the table to try to catch the tail end of the story.

But it wasn't okay. Even knowing that she put the homework in my backpack did not calm me down. Instead, my feelings intensified. I needed to get home *right* now. This was no longer fun —I needed to get to my homework immediately.

Somewhere between third and fourth grade, I had developed a deep, unrelenting fear that my homework was not in my backpack. I do not know where this fear came from, but it was there, and it was constant.

The next hour was agonizing. My teammates continued to play in the arcade, my parents continued to drink and eat pizza in the red booths, and I continued to panic.

When we finally got home, I made a beeline straight to the kitchen. My backpack hung from the nail, slightly agape. I saw the red folder and grabbed it immediately. I opened it up and peered inside and confirmed what my mom had told me an hour earlier— that she had put my homework in my backpack. Not only was it there, but it was completed and ready to turn in the next day.

"See, I told you I put it away!" Mom said as she saw me zip the backpack back up.

"Thanks," I muttered and headed to my room.

Later, as I lay in bed trying to sleep, I could hear my parents' voices fluttering down the hallway. The panic began to rise again, and a few minutes later I found myself creeping down the hallway, back into the kitchen toward my backpack.

The voices stopped.

"Sasha, what are you doing up?" Dad said. "Do you need some water?"

"No, I just needed to check my backpack."

"Your backpack? For what?"

"My homework. I am not sure if it's in there," I responded, my shaky voice giving away my uneasy feelings.

"We already did that, Sasha," Mom chimed in. "Remember? We checked it when we got home from the game."

I did remember. But it didn't help.

"Well, let me just check one more time," I insisted.

This happened three more times before I finally went to bed.

FOR YEARS, I'd lie in my bedroom at night after the lights had gone out, straining my eyes to make out the shapes of furniture in my room. The heavy white desk with brass handles painted gold; I could hear how they would clink each time I opened a drawer. Through the darkness, I could make out the outlines of the built-in shelves along the foot of my bed which held the American Girl Doll books stacked neatly in a corner. I snuggled my Beauty and the Beast pillow and rested my cheek on the cool pillowcase, adorned by Belle's face— I would never *ever* flip the pillow over. I wouldn't dare let my face rest on the side with the Beast on it. It didn't matter that he was the kind Beast, the one in the blue dress suit waltzing with Belle. I couldn't let the Beast touch my face or else bad things might happen.

As the years went on, my pillowcase and sheets changed, but my behavior did not. After lying in bed long enough to let my eyes adjust to the darkness, I'd bolt out of bed and start the long walk down the hall. There, at the end of my walk, I would find it: my backpack.

Over the years, different versions of the same JanSport backpack hung from the same sturdy nail, secured below the white tile counter in our kitchen. Slowly, I'd unzip my backpack, look at my completed homework, and trudge back to my bedroom to begin the loop again.

IT WAS Christmas morning and Santa had left us a huge, heavy box. Glitter littered the carpet as we ripped off the gold and maroon wrapping paper. Dad bent over and lit the match to ignite the Duralog in the fireplace. Mom sat on the gold and maroon chair with her tan legs wrapped beneath her. She sipped her coffee, probably wondering how many more years she would have before we noticed that she and Santa liked the same colors.

The maroon and gold paper fell to the ground and revealed two new colors: black and white spots adorned the box, the cow design instantly connecting in our brains.

"It's a computer!" we squealed.

Our very own computer for our house.

We must be millionaires, I thought.

Our parents set up our new Gateway computer in the spare bedroom, which would eventually become my mom's home office. Dad would use the computer at nighttime. Years later, he would swear that he had thought of the idea of e-Bay before anybody else, but he just didn't know how to do computer programming. Millionaires were always stealing Dad's ideas, it seemed.

One evening, Dad sat tinkering on the computer. The bright light of the screen illuminated his face in contrast to the darkness of the room. My sister and I lay on the stiff futon mattress, craning our heads to see the tiny TV that sat high above Dad's head in the corner of the room.

"Shhh," Dad suddenly hushed us, using his large hands to peel apart the blinds and peek out the window.

"Oh no you don't!" he said to himself as he jumped up, knocking the chair back.

"Stay here and don't move!" he instructed as he ran down the hallway in his tighty-whities and white V-neck, heading straight out the front door. He didn't bother to close it.

What felt like hours later, he returned home breathing slightly heavier. "Okay girls, time for beddie-bye!" he said as he bent down and scooped us up one by one and brought us to our beds.

The next morning when I went outside to play, I saw graffiti sprawled all over our front wall. *Who would have done that? Why would someone graffiti our house? Are we in danger?* I thought with a bit of panic. Then I remembered what Dad said last night as he was tucking me in: "Don't worry, I got the guys. Nobody outruns your Dadio."

Years later, I learned the full story, or at least the version Dad wanted to tell me: a group of kids were spray-painting on our freshly painted white wall. Dad heard the rattle of the spray paint cans and ran outside. When the kids heard the tinkling of the bell on our front door, they took off. But they were no match for Dad. He chased them down the street barefoot and, in his underwear, tackled them and told them never to come back again. I wouldn't be surprised if they gave up spray-painting for good after that.

WHEN I WAS twelve years old, Dad took us to Yosemite to climb Half Dome. We did no training whatsoever. Dad decided it would be a fun thing to do, so one weekend we just showed up. We stayed in the tent cabins, and Dad had let me bring along my best friend, Catherine. She was like our third sister—she came with us everywhere.

We set out early in the morning, the mist dangling in our hair and clouding our view as we marched forward. The fog helped to hide the treacherous trail that lay before us. We had one water bottle each and my mom's backpack held a few turkey sandwiches and some oranges. Dad believed in packing light.

Stopping to rest at Half Dome

Eventually, the fog began to lift from the sky and from our minds, and we realized that this hike was substantially harder than Dad had prepared us for. We cried as we climbed the thousands of stairs up the side of the Vernal Falls waterfall. I could not enjoy the beautiful scenery because I was so exhausted. My legs burned with muscle fatigue and my eyes burned with tears, but Dad forged ahead. He was always twenty yards in front of us. He would look back to make sure nobody had fallen off a cliff, encourage us to keep going, and then turn back around and continue hiking. Mom was left to corral the three of us and deal with our whining and crying.

After approximately four hours of hiking, I began to feel dizzy and lightheaded. My fingers were swelling, and my nose started to bleed.

"Boris, we need to stop!" Mom called out. "Sasha's nose is bleeding."

"A little blood never hurt anybody—plus, we're almost to the top!" Dad replied.

"I'm dizzy!" I shouted. My head grew clammy, and I sat on a jagged rock.

"She cannot go any further. We have to turn around," Mom argued.

"Okay, if you turn around and go back about a quarter mile, you can take the kids and go eat those sandwiches by the water in a shady spot," Dad directed. "We are almost to the cables, so I am going ahead and I will meet you at the water in about an hour." He turned and marched forward.

Sometimes, our childhood memories are warped—small molehills turned into treacherous mountains. This was not the case here. I recently reviewed the website for the National Park Service's instructions regarding Half Dome. According to the NPS: "The 14-to-16-mile round trip hike to Half Dome is not for you if you're out of shape or unprepared. Most hikers take 10 to 12 hours to hike to Half Dome and back; some take longer... a few visitors each summer have problems with altitude sickness. Symptoms may include severe headache and/or nausea. The only way to relieve altitude sickness is to descend immediately."

In Dad's mind, there was no reason why we couldn't ascend this mountain—all we had to do was put one foot in front of the other and climb! What was so hard about that? Time was irrelevant. Training? Not needed. Snacks? An extra luxury. While I admired his faith in our abilities, he didn't consider our upbringing and how it shaped us differently than his own.

Dad's famous mantras "Mind over matter" and "I love pain!" were funny to us, but they were real coping tools for him.

The pain of blisters and sore muscles was nothing to him—he had learned decades earlier how to block out much greater pains. The pains that come from growing up in poverty, as one of ten children of Russian and Finnish immigrants. At times, there wasn't enough food for all the children and Dad was forced to physically fight his five older brothers to get a few scraps of food. Often, the "food" consisted of rabbit their father had shot, the tiny carcasses full of buckshot.

I think back on my bloody nose and my blistered feet, and I am reminded of the piece of wood stuck in Dad's foot. At age eighteen, Dad was riding his motorcycle down Reseda Boulevard. As he approached a red light, he put his feet down on to the asphalt to slow himself and his bike. In that moment, a large stick shot up through the flimsy sole of his sneakers and rammed into the arch of his foot. The stick broke immediately, leaving a chunk of wood lodged in his foot. The remaining splinters sprinkled down around his shoe like discarded matchsticks.

Dad knew they didn't have money to waste on frivolous things like medical bills. And so, terrified of angering his mother, he simply taped up the bottom of his shoe and ignored it.

I imagine the wound festering and growing infected weeks later —red skin flaming around it and pus oozing out of the cracks in his sole. He ignored the wound long enough that eventually a new rough layer of skin grew over it, thick and calloused. But the wound never really healed.

Decades later, Dad would show us the piece of wood still lodged in his foot. I imagine the petrified piece of wood inside his foot, charred and dehydrated, like the trees throughout Yosemite that dried up and splintered in the summer months when water was sparse.

When we touched his foot, the wood jumped around, still distended in the fluid of his foot, threatening to burst out.

I wonder if they noticed this when he died. Did they tag his toe in the morgue and see that piece of wood, pushing through the skin of his foot? As he was cremated, did the piece of wood ignite, finally free after all those decades of being ignored?

PART II

6

GAPING WOUNDS

Senior year of high school, a sense of excitement and anticipation hung over every activity. I had never embraced change easily. I thrived on routine, on normalcy, on expectation. Senior year was emotionally challenging, for each activity brought with it a certain weight of being "the last." The last time I'd play in a volleyball match against our cross-town rivals, the Ventura Cougars. The last time I'd attend a high school football game with my friends. The last time I'd go to a high school dance. The last time I'd drive to the beach for a late-night bonfire with my group of high school friends.

I anticipated those lasts. What I didn't anticipate was the string of tragedies that would strike my family, wreaking havoc on my life and my emotional wellbeing for the next fifteen years.

2005 was the beginning of the end of my immediate family unit. As my family was bombarded with calamities, the cracks in the foundation of my parents' marriage grew into canyons. As we got hit by crisis after crisis, the only thing I knew how to do was to push forward, to keep going, to never stop.

NOVEMBER 2004, we hosted Thanksgiving at our house in Ventura. It wasn't often that we had Thanksgiving with Dad's side of the family. In fact, I couldn't even recall if we'd ever had Thanksgiving with all these family members together.

That year, both of Dad's sisters came, as did two of his brothers —Vlad and Nicoli. Did Dad know this would be the last Thanksgiving with those brothers when he scheduled the gathering? I will never know—I never asked him.

That day, when Nicoli and Betty arrived, Betty came up to me and said, "Do you know who I am? I am your Aunt Betty!" Sure, we didn't share holidays together often, but they weren't complete strangers. Of course, I knew who she was.

That is the only memory I have of that entire day: Aunt Betty introducing herself to me.

I look back on the photo of that day, and even that doesn't spark any memories. Sixteen of us sit on the porch, squinting at the camera. Are those squints because the sun was in our eyes, or because our smiles were forced?

Looking at the photo now is haunting—twenty years later, none of those families remain intact. Each branch shattered by divorce, disease and death.

Before the following Thanksgiving, both Nicoli and Vlad would be dead from colon cancer, and Dad would have received his first diagnosis. Did any of these smiling people know what was coming?

I WOKE up that morning and planned to go to the pier for a photo shoot with my friends. I put on jeans and a teal long-sleeved shirt with black piping around the collar. A dried rose and big sunglasses would complete the look I was going for—pensive and mysterious, but alluring.

Mom and Dad were gone, and I was gathering things for my photoshoot. To be clear, this was not a professional photoshoot. This was a photoshoot to get a new MySpace.com cover photo—much more important to a young teenager than a professional photoshoot.

I slipped on my brown chunky Reef sandals and got ready to head to the pier. And then, the house phone rang.

"Sasha, you and your sister need to come to the hospital," Mom said. "Uncle Nicoli isn't doing well."

"What? I am supposed to go to the pier with Catherine and Matt!" I protested in my perfect petulant teenage voice.

"Get your sister and come now. Put the hospital address into MapQuest.com, print the instructions, and come now."

As much as I wanted to completely blow off this request, I did as I was told. I was, after all, a perpetual rule-follower. And plus, her voice sounded extremely serious.

Launa and I loaded up into my white Jeep, the pink Roxy sticker shining off the back window, and headed for the 101 freeway. At that time, I had only been a licensed driver for a year and a half—this was the furthest I had ever driven by myself.

In Thousand Oaks, the gas light went on, but I didn't have time to stop. We needed to get there as soon as possible. I hoped I had enough gas to make it the rest of the way.

We arrived at the hospital and stepped out of the car. The air was sticky—unusually hot for January, even for the San Fernando Valley. As we approached the hospital, the automatic doors glided open and a *whoosh* of cold air hit us as we walked into a cloud of air conditioning.

"Um, we are here for Nicoli," I mumbled to the receptionist.

"Oh." She looked at me with sad eyes. "Let me get someone to take you to his room."

I thought we were going to see Uncle Nicoli in the hospital bed, sitting up, and talking to all of us. Launa and I had no idea what we were walking into. Even if we did, nothing could have prepared us for what we saw next.

We were ushered to the hospital room and chaos hit immediately. I struggled to orient myself to my surroundings.

Uncle Nicoli lay on the bed, his thin jaundiced body protruding from underneath an even thinner hospital blanket. Doctors and nurses crowded around the upper half of the hospital bed. Orange lights flashed, green lines bounced up and down on the screen around his body—numbers blinked, and people screamed as the doctors tried to seek instructions from family members on what to do next. "We need to make some decisions," the doctors said loudly. Nicoli's frail body shook as the doctors spoke to the adults in rushed voices.

The air conditioning blew forcefully out of the upper vents, but I was sweating profusely under the teal shirt that I had so carefully picked out for my photoshoot.

Someone screamed—was it me? With each shake of his body, my uncle's chest seemed to lift off the bed as if he were struggling to breathe.

I panicked. I had to get out of there.

I ran to the bathroom to try to escape the suffering that I was witnessing.

The florescent lights beamed down on me as I sat on the toilet and put my head in my hands, trying to figure out what to do next. I wanted to run away. To escape. *How did I get here?* My heart pounded and my breathing was heavy, as if I *had* been running.

But I couldn't escape.

"And though I walk through the Valley of the Shadow of Death, I fear no evil..." I heard my Dad's voice boom through the vent of the bathroom. *Where did he get a Bible? How did he know what parts to read? Was this what the Shadow of Death looks like?*

I stumbled back into the room only to be met with a grim realization: Uncle Nicoli was gone.

The screaming continued as family members crumpled on the linoleum floor in a tangle of arms and legs, sobbing hysterically. My dad, undeterred, continued to read from the Bible. Aunt Betty wailed. I don't remember what my mom was doing, but my sister and I stood by ourselves, paralyzed in fear, in a corner near the door.

Uncle Nicoli was gone.

"I'm so sorry," someone announced, as they led us out of the room and into another cold and empty room. We sat in stunned silence for what felt like hours until someone piped up—"Well, what should we get for lunch?"

Do people still eat lunch after watching someone die? I felt sick. Launa and I drove the whole way back to Ventura in silence. We didn't discuss what we had just seen or what it meant. Even though our bodies were physically close together, our already strong emotional walls were rapidly being fortified.

I stared ahead and let my mind wander. We were raised in the Christian faith. We had been taught to believe that God would provide for us and take care of us. But what kind of God would put our family through what we had just witnessed?

Of all his siblings, Dad was the closest to Uncle Nicoli. They shared a love of the simple things in life—swimming at the beach, camping and exploring nature. What kind of God would prematurely take away a good man and father, in front of his own family, no less? I didn't have a way to answer those questions. Maybe God just didn't care about us anymore, I decided. We woke up the next morning and went to school as if nothing out of the ordinary had happened.

Just keep moving, and you won't crash.

———

OUR FAMILY WAS TOUGH—PHYSICALLY, mentally, and emotionally. We were not whiners. We were not complainers. We suited up and showed up and did hard things. But something broke inside all of us that day, especially Dad. The death of Uncle Nicoli caused an irreparable shift in my dad, the effects of which would haunt us forever. The adventurous and generous Dad was still there, but we started to see a lot more of the angry and sullen Dad after Uncle Nicoli, his older brother, died. Truth be told, I don't think Dad ever recovered from the loss of his brother. I think Nicoli was the truest friend Dad ever had, and he lost his best friend that day.

By then, Dad had been in law enforcement for over a decade. He had seen his fair share of dead bodies and brutal crime scenes. He had already lost his mother, his father and two brothers by then. But this? This was different. After Nicoli died, Dad did everything he could to keep up the tough exterior—to maintain his physical and mental strength. But his emotional stability began to falter, and it only got worse. As we continued to face more tragedies head-on, he retreated into himself more and more.

IN THE DAYS AFTER A DEATH, all sense of normalcy evaporates. Schedules are abandoned and routines are forgotten.

I don't remember if it was evening or afternoon when I started talking to my mom about the logistics of the funeral and where Uncle Nicoli would be buried, but somehow, we found ourselves alone in the fancy living room.

"Will Uncle Nicoli be buried in the same place as Grandma and Grandpa?" I asked. Then I thought aloud, "Where are they buried, anyway?"

"No, he won't. I don't know where they are buried," Mom responded curtly.

"Oh. How come?"

Suddenly, a strange look came over Mom's face. Her lips parted to speak, but time froze as her mind raced to catch up. I could tell, in

STOPPING TO FEEL | 51

that moment, that she was struggling with how to answer. Contemplating what version of the story to tell me.

In the end, the truth prevailed.

"Your grandfather was a very bad man. He hurt a lot of people. He... well, he hurt children...physically, emotionally...sexually."

She paused for a moment, waiting for me to comprehend her words.

"He molested them. That's... well, that's why your father and I kept you girls away as much as possible. That's why we didn't see your grandparents much. That's why we didn't go to his funeral."

My mind flashed back to a few years earlier, when I learned that my grandpa had died. At the time, I had been heavily involved in club volleyball. My parents told me we wouldn't be attending the funeral because my grandfather would have wanted me to go to my volleyball tournament instead. I'd always found that answer strange —did he even know I played volleyball? I hadn't seen him in at least five years. But I had accepted the answer as truth and didn't question it. Now I wondered whether there even was a funeral to begin with.

Mom continued, "Your dad doesn't want you girls to know. He wants to keep it a secret. But I can't hold it any longer. It's wrong. It's awful." Her eyes misted and her voice cracked. "I have been sick to my stomach about it ever since I found out. After we first heard the news, your dad still visited his parents sometimes. I stay up late at night racking my mind to try and remember if we ever left you alone with him. If I ever took my eyes off you when we went to their house. If I ever... if I ever gave him an opportunity to hurt you."

First, confusion. *I don't understand. How is this happening? How can this be real?* My dad was a law enforcement officer. He supervised parolees who committed sex crimes. He interviewed them, tracked them and insisted they complied with the provisions of their parole. He made sure they stayed away from schools and registered with Megan's Law. How could his own *father* be a child molester? How could his father be like the men he supervised for a living? How could I be related to someone who had done something so horrific?

Then, a short moment of relief. I thought back to the few times we had visited the trailer in the desert. How my sister and I always played outside by ourselves while Dad went inside.

"No, Mom. I don't ever remember being alone with him."

She closed her eyes, leaned her head back, and exhaled a sigh of relief.

"When did this happen? How long have you known?" I asked.

"Since before you were born."

And then she began to share with me what she had been holding from me for so long:

In the late 1980s, before I was born, my dad applied for numerous law enforcement jobs. In 1985, he started working as a corrections officer at California Men's Colony in San Luis Obispo. The very first week of work, he heard someone yelling his name from across the yard. He turned and was shocked to see his older brother standing there. My dad, an officer; his brother, an inmate. Of course, my dad knew his older brother was in prison, but he didn't realize until that moment that his brother had been relocated to that same exact prison.

My uncle was transferred to another prison almost immediately. My grandmother was unhappy and blamed my father—now she would have to drive even further to visit my uncle in prison.

Not long after, my father transferred jobs and began working with low-risk prisoners in a fire camp in Southern California. The camp was a collaboration between the LA County Fire Department and the California Department of Corrections. My dad and other officers helped to train low-risk prisoners in how to fight fires.

The camp was directly across the highway from the canyon where my grandparents were now living in the single-wide mobile home.

What happened next was the beginning of the unraveling.

Shortly before I was born, several individuals started to come forward and accused my grandfather of sexually molesting them.

The news was a bombshell for my mom, who was currently pregnant and had a husband who was now working in his first "grown-up" job as a correctional officer.

To this day, I don't fully understand what happened after these victims came forward. But what I do know is this: my dad had just started a career in law enforcement and his father had just been accused of multiple sex crimes.

My dad didn't report it, and he forbade my mom from talking to him about it.

Each year that passed, another victim came forward, and another, and another. And still, nothing happened to my grandfather.

At first, my mom attempted to broach the subject with my dad, with disastrous results. He became angry and agitated. He refused to discuss it. He denied ever being a victim. But with what my mom had heard, she didn't believe it possible that he had been spared.

Where I have clear and vivid memories of Uncle Nicoli's death, my memories of this night with Mom are fuzzier. I remember the stories she told me, but otherwise, my memories come to me as feelings, rather than visions. Confusion. Disgust. Disbelief. Relief. Sadness. Fear. But most of all, shame.

How could this be part of my family's story? How could this be? How, how, how? What about the love story of how my grandparents met in the barn while my grandfather was in hiding from the Russians? What about the fabulous story about my grandparents coming to America? What about all the stories my dad had told me about them? I shared DNA with this man. Those stories made up who I was as a human being. How on earth did this one fit in?

I was proud of my Russian heritage. In fact, local high school sports commentators had nicknamed me "the Crushin' Russian" after witnessing how hard I could hit a volleyball. But my connection to my Russian heritage was through my grandfather. How could I continue to honor that part of my heritage after I learned these horrible things about him?

How could I continue to enjoy the tale of my grandparents' love story now that I knew it didn't have a happy ending? Worst yet—that my own grandfather was the villain?

ALTHOUGH WE GREW up in the Presbyterian church, in recent years I had started to pull away. I was weary of the youth pastors' inability to answer some of my questions. As I started to develop normal teen curiosities around boys, alcohol and (mild) rebellion, going to church only brought up feeling of guilt in me. I felt judged, out of place, unconnected. I never seemed to experience those "miracle moments" that everyone else experienced. I asked God to show himself to me, and he didn't.

For years, although we went to church on Sundays and youth group on Wednesdays, I didn't feel like we were really a part of the church. We went through the motions of going to church and being involved, but I never felt like the teachings sunk into the core of our being like it did for our other church friends. We didn't know Bible verses by heart, and we often forgot to pray before dinner. I felt like we were fakes. We never measured up to the "real" Christians who went to church with us.

As our lives got busier with sports and weekend commitments, we missed more and more church. Although, truthfully, I had been mentally checking out of church for a while. I didn't have any reason to believe that God was watching out for me and my family anymore. Why should I keep going? Even still, my parents still tried to keep our connection intact, insisting that we at least go on the major holidays. Somehow, we had slowly become C&E Christians.

On Easter Sunday, March 27, 2005, I woke up and begrudgingly began to get ready for church. I don't remember what I was wearing, or what we had planned to do after church. All I remember is what happened next.

Dad told me and Launa to meet him in Launa's bedroom for a talk. As soon as I walked in the room, I could feel that something was wrong. My body physically tensed as my mind raced. I quickly tried to observe everything and anticipate what was wrong. My sister sat cross-legged on her twin-sized bed. I looked around and made note of all the familiar things in her room. Her shelf sat eight inches from the ceiling of her bedroom and ran the length of the room. The shelf held countless softball trophies and medals. A bookshelf leaned against the wall, full of knick-knacks and *Lord of the Rings* novels. Dad sat at her white desk, looking handsome but stoic. His brown hair hung across his forehead, a few spare whisps lingering above his eyes. I tried to look past him but could not avoid his fierce blue eyes staring intently back at me.

"Mom will not be joining us at church today. Aunt Nancy had an accident, and Mom is going to drive to Kansas right away to be with her," he announced in a matter-of-fact tone.

"What? What happened?" someone said. Maybe it was me, I don't recall.

A pregnant pause.

"She tried to kill herself," a female voice blurted from behind me.

Until that moment, I didn't even know that Mom was in the room with us. I turned quickly and saw her—tears poured from her eyes as she leaned listlessly against the door jamb of Launa's bedroom door.

The words exploded out of Mom like emotional vomit she could not control. The tenor of her voice was an octave higher than usual. The truth had been sitting right behind her lips, waiting to rush out, like a secret that wasn't hers to keep.

Dad didn't go to her in that moment. He didn't comfort her, or us. Instead, we all stood in that room like four strangers conducting an arm's-length transactional business meeting. There was no discussion of emotions. There was no opportunity to share how it made us feel. There was no hugging or consoling. There was only the simple exchange of facts. And even then, we weren't originally given all the facts. The attempt to take one's life is a very intentional act, yet Dad had called it an "accident." He was always trying to shield us from the truth, to protect us from the pain.

If I felt disconnected from God before, I felt downright abandoned by him in that moment. It had barely been two months since we had witnessed the horror of Uncle Nicoli's death, and now my aunt had attempted suicide. Where was God and what was he doing to my family?

A journal entry from March 29, 2005, two days later:

Aunt Nancy is going to be ok. She is pretty much a miracle. They were going to pull the plug and now she is sitting up and talking. I am so happy. I don't think I could bear to see my mom go through that kind of pain. I guess she has amnesia and can't remember the last five years, which in my opinion, is a blessing, because apparently, they weren't very good ones...

A FEW MONTHS LATER, we were at an evening church event. We sat at large circular tables, each one covered by white butcher paper. Multicolored pens lay strewn about the center of each table. During the sermon, the pastor asked us all to grab a pen and draw a graph to represent how our relationship with God had changed over the last few months of attending the evening church program.

"As you witness the blessings God has placed in each of your lives, your faith in him should be increasing."

Out of the corner of my eye I watched as Mom grabbed a pen. A pool of ink formed on the white butcher paper as her hand hovered in the same spot for a minute. Then, she abruptly drew a line straight down before she covered her graph with her forearm so nobody could see.

But she wasn't quick enough—I saw it, and my heart sank. Even my parents' faith was failing.

7

TITANS TRAINING

Two months before I was supposed to leave for college, I received a letter in the mail from my coach.

Welcome to the Titans Volleyball Team! Enclosed please find your suggested summer training schedule to ensure that you are in top shape when you arrive for pre-season training in the fall... as part of your pre-season training, you will be tested on your ability to run the mile in under seven minutes.

Volleyball is a game of quick movements and short bursts of energy. It requires endurance for long rallies, but never more than fifteen or twenty feet of running. This prerequisite seemed absurd. Until that point, I had never run a mile under 8:15—how was I going to shave off over a minute in just two months?

Dad had been a runner my entire life. But not the kind of runner who suits up in moisture-wicking clothing and polarized Oakley sunglasses. No, Dad was the type of runner who shows up the day of the race in black gym shorts and a white cotton T-shirt, having just decided to register the week prior.

I told Dad about this new requirement for running the mile in under seven minutes.

He was not concerned in the slightest. "Running a mile under seven minutes is a piece of cake. We will do it tomorrow. Be ready in the kitchen by 8am—we want to finish training before it gets too hot."

Like most newly minted eighteen-year-olds, the last thing I wanted to do was run a mile at 8am at the beginning of summer vacation. But I never said no to Dad. Plus, how else was I going to learn how to run the mile that fast?

The next morning, I crawled out of bed, threw my hair in a ponytail, and stumbled toward the car. I should have known Dad would have other plans.

"Start walking—it's our warm-up!"

We walked in silence to the high school. I was almost as tall as Dad by then, but he was still always two full leg lengths in front of me. This wasn't a social walk; we had a mission to accomplish.

A few minutes later, we arrived at the field where just two weeks earlier I had walked across the stage to receive my diploma. I hadn't expected to return to my alma mater so quickly.

Dad took his place at the 100m line on the right-hand side of the track. "What time do you need to beat?" he asked.

"Seven minutes."

"Okay, we can do that."

I looked at Dad. He was not wearing a watch or holding a stopwatch. .

"I have been running for thirty years—I know what a seven-minute mile feels like. I don't need no stinkin' stopwatch," he boasted. "Trust me. Just stay with me—right by my side—and we will get it done."

Ten seconds later, we were off. Dad's powerful legs pushed forward with ease, but I struggled to keep up. I sucked in shallow breaths as we rounded every corner. My legs grew feeble as I started to fall behind him.

"Stay with me, Boomer!" he hollered over his shoulder. "All you have to do is stay with me."

"I'm trying, but I'm tired!" I gasped as a sharp pain ripped up my side.

"Remember what I said, just trust me!"

I stared at the back of his white shirt and fixated on the words *Baker to Vegas*, the run he did through Death Valley every year. If I just focused on being able to read those words, I knew I would never be too far behind him.

He pushed me around each corner, never slowing down, only encouraging me to keep up.

"Come on, you can do it—one more corner!" he shouted. "We are almost done."

The sun burned my eyes as I rounded that last corner. The 100m mark where we had started was in my sight. My legs felt like rubber and acid churned in my stomach.

I crossed the 100m mark and stumbled ten more feet to the turf, where I promptly fell to my knees, threw up stomach bile and rolled to my back, my forearm shielding my eyes from the cruel morning sun.

I heard the crunch of the turf as Dad walked over. I moved my arm to the side and squinted to see him reaching his long arm down to pull me up.

After he helped me to my feet, he pulled a watch out of his pocket to show me. "6:58. I knew you could do it." So he *did* have one after all.

Then he turned to start walking home.

As I was working on strengthening my body that summer, my uncle Vlad's body was deteriorating. The colon cancer continued to ravage his body. Dad was still reeling from the death of his brother Nicoli in January, but he avoided dealing with it by focusing his energy on his brother Vlad's treatment.

At first, after Nicoli died, Dad wanted to keep the death from Vlad. He thought that if Vlad learned their other brother hadn't survived the disease they were both fighting, it would kill his spirit. Dad drove to and from Lompoc to see Vlad all the time. He visited the hospital, delivered supplies and spoke to the doctors.

One day, after Vlad had been discharged from a recent hospital stay, Dad loaded up our family to go visit him and his wife Sue, along with their four children. Although they lived only an hour away, I have very few childhood memories of visiting them. My cousins were much older than me, and I was always intimidated by their intelligence. Their eldest son literally studied astrophysics at Harvard. I didn't dare even speak to him for fear of sounding idiotic.

This entire visit was extremely uncomfortable. Vlad's lumbering figure had whittled down to a mere 180 pounds. He sat propped in a recliner chair in the front room. Memories of that day come to me in flashes—jumbled and confused. Muted browns and grays. Afghan blankets. Orza pasta with artichokes, cherry tomatoes, and feta. The starchy smells of lunch barely masked the sterile smell of medical equipment hidden throughout the room. We sat in the living room around the ailing man in his recliner. I looked out the window to avoid eye contact. A steep slope down the backyard. Dried plants and hot air. Was that causing my suffocation, or was it imagined?

The adults tried to act cheery, like this was a normal visit on a normal day. But it was anything but normal. Underneath the façade was the reality that Vlad was lying there dying, right in front of our eyes, just like Nicoli had months earlier. The only difference was that Vlad's decline was slower, more labored, more drawn-out.

Dad spent the afternoon bragging about me and Launa, as he

normally did. He told Vlad about our sports accomplishments and my future at Cal State Fullerton. I stared out the window, embarrassed, per usual. Wishing I was anywhere but there.

But then Vlad said something that has stuck with me for the rest of my life. It's hard to describe why this one simple sentence meant so much to me, but as our family continued to experience chaos over the next several years, I clung to his words like a life raft keeping me afloat. This uncle I barely had a relationship with helped to shape the next decade of my life in a way he probably never imagined—or, frankly, intended.

"You are in control of your education," he said. "Don't ever take it for granted."

Control. I could have it. Control. It could be mine. Control. When everything else around me was crumbling—I could have my education. My studies. My school.

I could have Control.

Vlad died a few weeks after that visit, and I spent the next decade throwing all my energy into my education and professional accomplishments under the false sense of security that Control provided.

8

CANCER COMES HOME

My boyfriend Rob and I had been long-distance dating for a year—I moved away to Orange County for college, and he stayed in Ventura to attend Ventura College. At the time, he was working at Longs Drugs as a stock room receiver: unload pallets. Stock shelves. Repeat.

That summer evening, he was anxious to get off work, as I had just come back to town for summer break. He was in the back of the store, unloading pallets of merchandise and joking with his coworkers, when suddenly he heard a familiar voice call out, "Helllllo, is Robbie back here? Helloooo!" His ears perked up as he tried to place the voice—it wasn't his manager or a coworker, but it was recognizable.

He figured it out a moment later when Dad came slinking around the corner. Dad was a formidable figure. Not only was he over six feet tall and discreetly muscular, but he was fast. He moved around slyly, like a cat waiting to pounce.

Rob was shocked to see his girlfriend's father not only at his work, but in the back part of the store reserved for employees only. It was there, in that dusty Long's drugstore stockroom amongst discarded piles of soda and bags of chips, that Dad told Rob he had cancer.

At the same time Dad was cornering Rob in the back of the stockroom, I was sitting in the kitchen of my house having a fight with my mom. I wanted to go out with Rob and friends that night, but she insisted I stay home for a family dinner. I couldn't even remember the last time we had a family dinner and didn't understand why she was deciding to start coordinating one now. But she was firm and unwavering. I could not go out. I would stay home for family dinner, there were no two ways about it.

I stormed off to my bedroom to sulk and wait for Rob to call me when he got off work. About thirty minutes later, my pink Motorola flip phone started to chirp with Rob's familiar ringtone. I answered and immediately told him how my parents were being rude and not allowing me to go out that night.

Rob responded with hesitation, "So, you talked to your dad then?"

I had not, and I didn't know what Rob was talking about—why did he care whether I had spoken to my dad that evening? He tried desperately to play it off as general curiosity and change the subject, but I wasn't having it. I forced him to tell me what was going on.

It was then that Rob blurted out, "Your Dad has cancer. He came to my work and told me a little while ago—I thought he would have told you by now."

I was stunned. Despite everything that had happened to our family over the last year, when my mom insisted we have a family dinner, I did not expect they had bad news to share. How could Dad have cancer? How could this be? He already got tested after his brothers died and he was clear. How could the cancer have come on so quickly since then?

Mom knocked on my door and asked if I was ready to come to dinner. When she opened my door, my eyes were red-rimmed and my face was angry.

"How could you not tell me Dad has cancer!?" I fired at her.

She looked at me, puzzled. How did I know? The whole point of the family dinner was for Dad to tell me and Launa at the same time. But Dad always had secret plans, and telling Rob was one of them.

Mom and I walked to the dinner table together, me crying, with my arms folded tightly over my chest. Mom following close behind, shooting messages at Dad with her eyes, the way people who have been married for twenty years can do so efficiently.

Launa was the only one who didn't know yet. She was only sixteen.

Dad's face was set in his typical stoic look—blue eyes bursting out of a face as unmoving as stone. No emotions on display.

He cleared his throat. "Well, your old Dadio went and got another colonoscopy, and it turns out I have colon cancer also. But don't worry, it's not as bad as Nicoli and Vlad's... we caught it early."

I looked down at my plate and poked at my food. Small grains of white Minute Rice stuck to my fork like putty.

He continued, "I am going to have surgery at UCLA to remove the section of my large intestine where the polyps are, and I shouldn't even need chemo or radiation!"

Nobody except Dad ate much that night.

A FEW WEEKS LATER, we drove down to UCLA for Dad's surgery. We stayed the night in a hotel connected to the hospital. To lighten the mood, we went to see *Pirates of the Caribbean* that night—as if Johnny Depp's swashbuckling around a bunch of pirates and scantily-clad maidens could distract us from the fact that Dad was having an operation to remove a cancerous part of his body the next day. I don't know why we went to the movies—Dad never liked movies, anyway.

The next day, we woke up early and traveled across the street to the hospital. Dad checked in and went back to the pre-op room, while we were forced to stay and wait in the main lobby. The surgery was scheduled to last for four hours. At hour three, I began to get restless and walked outside to find some food. I figured the walk and the food would be a good distraction for the upcoming fourth hour when the surgery would be over and we'd be able to go see Dad.

But after I got back, the fourth hour came and went, as did the fifth. Finally, five and a half hours after the surgery started, a doctor came out to meet with Mom. He told her there had been a complication in the surgery. They had performed the entire surgery and had sewn Dad back up, only to realize that they had missed a part of the cancer and needed to do the entire surgery again.

Normally, they would send the patient to post-op for recovery and schedule an additional surgery. However, since Dad was in extraordinarily good physical condition, they decided not to wake him up and send him to post-op. Instead, they decided to keep him under general anesthesia long enough to perform a *second* surgery. What should have been a four-hour surgery turned into a twelve-hour surgery.

Although Dad's vitals were good, they did not properly account for how much anesthesia they would need to keep such a man anesthetized. Halfway through the second surgery, Dad's eyes sprung open. When he realized he was strapped to a metal table, he began to panic. He thrashed around, trying to extricate himself from the table—his midsection still wide open. Scalpels and tools fell to the floor as the hospital staff were forced to subdue him.

We later learned that the "minor complication" was a major error. The doctors performing the surgery had removed the wrong portion of Dad's large intestine. Instead of removing the cancerous part, they removed an entire section of healthy intestines and completely missed the cancer. They had completed the four-hour surgery without even touching the cancerous part of the intestine.

Later, Mom and Dad consulted with a medical malpractice attorney regarding the botched surgery. It turns out, colons are not worth very much money, so the lawyer declined to take their case. My parents never sought a second opinion. Dad was just happy to finally have the right part gone and to make it out alive.

DESPITE THE COMPLEXITY of the surgery, the hospital discharged Dad just a few days later. Dad sat in the recliner in his bedroom as blood and pus seeped out of his stomach and soaked his white T-shirt. The wet shirt clung to the metal staples that were supposed to be holding his flesh together.

"This is not right. I should not be oozing this much."

"Maybe we just need the nurse to come and re-pack it?" Mom suggested.

"Kelly," Dad responded curtly. "I've been involved in enough cancer treatments to know when something isn't right. A little extra gauze isn't going to help me. Get me back to UCLA, now."

Mom did as she was told and loaded Dad up in the car and drove him back to UCLA—an hour drive from our house.

Dad was right: his wound had reopened, and he was leaking fluid everywhere. When Mom got him to UCLA, they ended up having to admit him so they could remove and then reapply all the sutures to the wound and give him fluids and antibiotics to ward off any infections. Mom stayed in LA with him and so, for the first time ever, I was home alone in an empty house for a few days.

At nineteen years old, I decided to seize the moment and invite some friends over for a "small gathering." As these things always do, this "small gathering" ballooned into a larger group than I had anticipated. My feeling of being the "cool girl throwing the house party" lasted approximately five minutes. I was so anxious and worried about getting in trouble or someone spilling or misplacing a couch cushion that I couldn't relax the whole night. I walked from room to room, making sure people weren't putting their feet on the coffee tables or smashing Mom's fancy pillows in the formal living room. Those fancy pillows were already the topic of awkward conversation, seeing as how they were adorned with tiny naked cherubs and their tiny naked penises.

I had tried to mask my unease about the situation with Dad by surrounding myself with friends and a house party. Instead, they ended up making it worse. There wasn't anybody I felt comfortable talking to about it that night, but I also couldn't bring myself to let loose and enjoy myself since I was so worried about getting in trouble. I was also riddled with guilt—what kind of girl throws a house party when her dad is in the hospital? It was the first and last time I threw a house party.

"Ho, Ho, Ho, Merrrrrrrrry Christmas!" Dad called out as he hobbled through the burgundy front door. That sentence was quintessential Dad, and one of life's greatest mysteries. Every month of the year *except* December, Dad would randomly use that sentence to announce his presence when he came home. We never knew why he did it, but it came to symbolize his being home. The big man was in the house again.

And so, with Dad back from the hospital with new sutures in place, we started the healing process once again. But just like last time, things would not go exactly as planned.

Just a few days after Dad returned home from UCLA for the second time, Grandpa Bud, Mom's father, fell very ill. Grandpa Bud had been living with debilitating multiple sclerosis for decades. He had been confined to a motorized scooter for all my life. After being in a nursing home for a few weeks, they discharged him back home for hospice. Mom had barely returned from UCLA when she had to shift focus and fly to Montana to be with her own father in his final days. She left us at home with Dad and his festering stomach wound.

WHILE MOM WAS FLYING to Montana and Dad was confined to his recliner, I was still trying to think of ways to make the most out of my summer vacation. I walked around in circles in my backyard, attempting to get a tan while texting friends to coordinate plans.

Whoosh! The back window opened, and Dad hollered for me to come grab the house phone—Mom was on the line and needed to talk to me.

Irritated, I went inside and grabbed the phone. Mom immediately started talking in a rushed voice: "The end is near... Say goodbye... I will hold the phone."

I heard only fragments of her sentences as I tried to piece together the rest. Grandpa Bud was going to die that day, and I should say goodbye. I understood what she was saying, but I had no idea how to do what she was asking. I gripped the phone awkwardly, not sure what to expect. Would I hear talking? Breathing? Would he respond?

"Go ahead," Mom urged in a terse whisper.

"Oh, well, um, I am sorry you aren't feeling good, Grandpa. Love you, and umm, you were a good grandpa, and umm okay, goodbye." I hung up abruptly, not wanting to find out if I had been on speakerphone or not.

A week later, me, Dad, Launa, and our great-aunt Carolyn loaded into the Big Green Van and headed for Montana for the funeral. The Big Green Van had transported us to many adventures over the years, from softball tournaments to proms, but this was its first multi-state funeral road trip.

Dad was unable to drive. He sat in the passenger seat, reclining at a forty-five-degree angle so as not to upset the wound running across his abdomen.

From the passenger seat, he directed me and Launa as we took turns driving twenty-seven hours straight to Montana. We didn't have time or money to waste on frivolous things like flights and hotels.

Great-Aunt Carolyn sat in the backseat, knitting the whole way. She never drove—not because she couldn't, but probably because she was too scared of Dad. From his place in the passenger seat, he aggressively barked directions at whichever one of us was driving. Launa had only been a licensed driver for a few months. She hugged the steering wheel and barely pushed the Big Green Van to fifty miles an hour. As we inched through the desert outside of Las Vegas, Dad yelled that she was going to get us all killed by going so slow. Driving *too* slowly is not an insult you typically hear launched at a teenager.

I tried to drown out the fighting with Taking Back Sunday in my headphones, but it was hard to hear over the 70s classic rock that Aunt Carolyn insisted we play on the van stereo. It was not a peaceful or enjoyable trip—I wanted to get there as soon as possible so the tension in the car would end. But getting to our destination meant arriving at yet another funeral, so I wasn't exactly excited to get there either.

This definitely wasn't how I had envisioned spending my first summer back from college.

By then, I had stopped telling people everything that was going on with my family. I didn't know how to ask for, or accept, help. I didn't know how to express my feelings, and I felt unworthy of people's sympathies. Surely, we had worn them all out with everything that happened in 2005. How could I tell them something *else* had happened? And so, I mostly kept it to myself. Of course, I told Rob because he was my boyfriend, but I didn't tell the girls on my volleyball team, or my roommates or my high school friends. I tried to blow it off like it was no big deal that we were driving two states away to another funeral just days after my dad had been released from the hospital after having his cancerous colon removed.

At Grandpa Bud's funeral – Dad's stomach is probably still oozing under this shirt.

9

MAINTAINING CONTROL

When faced with traumatic experiences, some people turn to drugs, alcohol, or promiscuity. I turned to academics. I had always done well in school, but after the slew of deaths started in 2005 and that offhand comment from Uncle Vlad, I became hyper-focused on my education.

I had chosen to attend college at Cal State Fullerton to play volleyball. Sports had long been a physical and emotional outlet for me, a place where I thrived and enjoyed myself. I was thrilled to have achieved my goal of being recruited to play Division I college volleyball. But instead of volleyball serving as an avenue of relieving stress – my college volleyball career became a new and unexpected *source* of stress.

I had played team sports since I was a young girl. I was no stranger to new teammates, new coaches, new gymnasiums and new ways of playing. I knew the game like the back of my hand. But my place on this new team never felt secure. I constantly doubted myself. I worried that I wasn't good enough. I made simple mistakes during practice and then mentally beat myself up over it for days on end.

Halfway through the season, I accidentally stepped on a sewing needle while shuffling to the bathroom in the middle of the night. When I mentioned that my foot was hurting in practice that week, my coaches taped my foot up with Ace bandages and I continued to practice.

But weeks went on and my foot continued to throb. One morning I woke up and noticed red lines snaking up my calves and realized I couldn't put pressure on it. The arch of my foot was completely red and swollen. I set my foot up on the bathroom counter and tried to look at it more closely. I pressed gently on the arch of my foot and – *PING*!! A half-inch long needle shot out of the bottom of my foot and hit the bathroom faucet.

Apparently, when I stepped on the needle a month before, half of it broke off inside the arch of my foot, causing a brutal infection.

After the needle incident, I was redshirted—killing my chances of playing at all that year. The only thing more embarrassing than being redshirted after stepping on a sewing needle was when I learned that my dad had called my coach and read her the riot act for not believing I was really injured, forcing me to continue practicing and allowing my foot to become badly infected.

After that, rather than leaning harder into volleyball to overcome this minor setback, I began to feel that my future as a college athlete was slipping away from me. There were too many variables for it to feel in my sphere of control anymore.

While my volleyball career seemed to be unmanageable, my education was different—I was the only one who had the ability to show up for myself. School was the one thing I felt I could control at that point. I, and I alone, had the ability to determine the outcome of each exam, each paper, each class. So I read all the books, completed all the extra-credit work, went to all the "optional" events, and visited professors during office hours.

At one point, towards the end of the season, my coach asked me to come to her office. She expressed her condolences that I was being redshirted that year but commended me for bringing up the grade point average for the entire team. She noticed that I had the highest GPA of anybody on the team and asked if I could bring it up even higher the following semester. If I had a higher grade point average, that would bring up the overall average for the team— essentially overcompensating for my teammates who were struggling in school.

"Of course!" I said without hesitation. Never mind that I was drowning in my own work, or that I thought it was preposterous to have to do even better with my grades to make up for the poor grades of some of my teammates—if that's what I was asked to do, I would do it.

Even though I was redshirted, I was still an active member of the team, which meant showing up for practice several hours a day, five days a week. In the mornings, we'd lift weights and run laps around the soccer stadium for conditioning. In the afternoons, we'd meet in the gym to practice for another two hours. All those hours of training and practicing were hours that I wasn't able to study. Soon, my fixation with academics outweighed my love of the game, and I decided to quit the team.

The funny thing is that despite my obsession with excelling in school and the accolades to prove it, I still never believed I was that smart. I always worried that I was going to fail a class, or that I was totally wrong in my analysis of an issue, or that I hadn't studied enough. This self-doubt was all internal and stemmed from fear, not from lack of support. My dad was my biggest cheerleader, and my parents always told me and my sister how smart we were, and how we could achieve anything.

But this need to control, this need to excel, the need to be busy was so deeply ingrained in me that I knew no other way.

Even though I made the choice to quit the team to further my own academic goals, I still felt a deep sense of loss. I lost the connection with my teammates and I felt that I lost my identity as an athlete. Since I had chosen to attend Cal State Fullerton solely for athletics, once I quit the team I felt very out of place on campus. I stuck it out at Cal State Fullerton for another year, before I decided to transfer to the University of California, Santa Barbara for my junior and senior years.

10

CRABGRASS AND TALKING BACK

W hat do you do when you learn that the person who raised you to follow a certain standard of ethics and guided your entire moral compass in life, doesn't follow his own rules? What do you do when you learn that the man who taught you about compound interest and having multiple streams of income, is barely scraping by financially?

Was Dad full of shit the entire time? Why did he not follow his own advice?

After Dad died, every single person who learned of his death reached out to tell me how proud he was of me and Launa, and our children. Every single person told me that we were the most important things to him in the entire world. I believe this to be true —and yet, he made so many decisions that were just so damaging to his children, sometimes it's hard to wrap my head around. Did he really believe the decisions he was making wouldn't hurt us, or did he not care? These are the questions for which I will never have an answer. Sometimes I am at peace with that, and sometimes it haunts me.

It was the summer before I transferred to UCSB to finish college. I left behind my dreams of being a Division I volleyball star at Cal State Fullerton and moved back home for the summer before starting school in Santa Barbara. Dad decided I should get a job at the Santa Barbara Police Department. I never stopped to wonder if that is what I wanted—I just went with it because he told me to do it.

He insisted I apply for the job as soon as possible so that I could "get my foot in the door" and start a state pension. He was always waxing poetic about state pensions and compounding interest.

So, while my friends were blending smoothies at Jamba Juice and stacking books in local libraries, I was signing up to undergo a six-month-long background check so I could work in a police department.

Dad gave me the application. I was a mere nineteen years old— there were more pages in that application than there were years in my life. I took it to the desk in my room and dutifully filled it out—I listed everywhere I had lived for the past ten years, provided all my neighbor's names and my credit history. Then, I got to the section about drug usage.

Have you ever used illegal drugs, including but not limited to marijuana, cocaine, heroin, methamphetamine, and prescription drugs not prescribed to you?

NOTE: use of illegal drugs will not disqualify you from employment. However, dishonesty may be grounds for disqualification.

My pen hovered over the paper and my heart began to race.

I had never been interested in drugs—the D.A.R.E. program had instilled in me a sufficient fear of them. Plus, Dad was a parole officer. I couldn't do drugs!

But, one night in the summer right after my high school

graduation, the pressures of young love had worn me down. Against my better judgment, I decided to try smoking weed. Rob and I had just started dating, and he insisted I would love it—"Trust me, you will feel so relaxed, and the music will sound so cool!"

He picked me up for a date in his beat-up Toyota Tacoma, the red paint chipping off the sides. He opened the door for me from the inside—not to be chivalrous, but because the outside door handle was broken.

We drove to a secluded part of town and parked in the back of the parking lot, where the streetlights didn't reach. He pulled out the small pipe and packed it with dried leaves. The sweet smell of marijuana mixed with burnt residue instantly propelled me back to high school parties and the gang of kids that huddled around each other outside. I always avoided those huddles.

I took the pipe and inhaled, waiting for the rush of relief that he told me to expect. But I felt nothing.

I tried again.

"Whoa, slow down, you need to wait a minute for it to hit," he cautioned.

He turned the music up and we closed our eyes. The screech of the electric guitar amplified in my mind as it began to wander. What was I doing? Where was the relief?

"This doesn't feel good. I thought it was supposed to feel cool?" I panicked as I felt my head floating a few feet above my body, while my legs stayed cemented to the passenger seat.

"Shit, maybe we shouldn't have done this on an empty stomach. Let's go grab some food."

I didn't want to risk running into anybody that we knew, so I insisted we go to a place we had never been before. We arrived at the run-down diner and the rows of empty booths confirmed we were in the right place. Nobody else was voluntarily going to DW's Steakhouse for a Friday night date.

We sat at a table, and he tried to talk to me, but his words were miles away. All I could focus on were the circus animals behind him. Elephants, lions, and zebras paraded through the dirty plexiglass that divided our table from the one behind it.

"You folks ready to order?" the waitress chirped.

I almost jumped out of my seat. But I couldn't speak—I was too mesmerized by the plexiglass animals.

After being met with an awkward silence, she muttered, "Okay, I will give you folks a few more minutes with the menu and come back." As if the menu was the issue.

"Umm, are you okay?" Rob whispered as he leaned over across the table toward me.

"No. I don't know what's going on—I should have never done this. We're going to get in trouble. I need you to call my mom right now."

"I'm not calling your mom," he hissed. "Are you crazy? She'll never let me take you out again!"

"Fine, don't call her. But we better leave before the waitress calls her first!"

"Chill out—that's not going to happen. We don't even know this waitress, and this waitress doesn't know your mom."

All the reasoning in the world was not enough to convince me, and he could see that this marijuana experiment was not going the way he had planned. He didn't want me to panic anymore, and so he agreed to leave without any food. We went back to the car, where we sat for hours, as he calmed my fears and talked me out of calling my mom.

"Well, we're never doing that again," he confirmed.

Eventually, he dropped me off at home where I collapsed into bed and managed to fall asleep, and in the morning I felt normal again.

A year later, I stared at the job application and wondered how to answer.

Nervously, I told my mom what I had done and asked her what

to do about the question on the application. Of course, she recommended I ask my dad, since he was the one encouraging me to apply for the job in the first place.

I dreaded having that conversation with Dad, so I took the easy way out and left the application on the kitchen counter with a sticky note on the page inquiring about drug usage.

Dad, I tried smoking pot one time. I'm sorry. How should I answer this question? I scribbled on the sticky note.

Days went by and the job application stayed on the counter. I was reminded of my shameful confession every time I walked through the kitchen. But I didn't dare bring it up with Dad—I was too scared. Scared of making him angry, but mostly scared of disappointing him.

Later that week, he finally brought it up.

"Hey Boomer... I saw your note about the application."

I gulped.

"I know you said in your note that you tried smoking pot... but, how do you know?"

I stared at him, confused. Was this a rhetorical question? But before I could answer, he continued.

"I mean, did you take it to a lab and test it before you smoked it? I doubt it. Therefore, you don't *know* that you smoked pot, right? For all you know, that was crabgrass you lit on fire."

I leaned against the doorway with my arms crossed tightly against my chest. I was sure of the words I was hearing, but less sure of what they meant.

"Why would you admit to something that you don't know for a fact is true?" And then he walked away.

A few weeks after I turned in the application, I had an in-person interview with a lieutenant.

"It says here on your application that you've never tried drugs, is that correct?" the tall lieutenant with the white-cropped hair said in a clipped voice.

"Yes, sir."

"Not even marijuana? That's a common thing for teenagers to experiment with—even cops' kids." He peered at me from across his desk.

My mind flashed to the conversation with Dad in the kitchen, and I struggled to push aside the images of the circus animals parading through the Plexiglas.

"No, not even marijuana," I responded.

Who knows what kind of pesticides they spray on crabgrass these days, I convinced myself.

TWO YEARS LATER, I was applying for a promotion within the police department. As part of that promotion, I would have to undergo an additional background check. By then, I had just begun to unravel the enigma that was my father. I was starting to become bolder in my attempts to separate myself from him. To think on my own and make decisions based on what I felt was right, not what Dad said to do.

> *Have you ever used illegal drugs, including but not limited to marijuana, cocaine, heroin, methamphetamine, and prescription drugs not prescribed to you?*
>
> *NOTE: use of illegal drugs will not disqualify you from employment. However, dishonesty may be grounds for disqualification.*

This time, I calmly checked the answer for "Yes."

Just like the first time I applied, I had my in-person interview a few weeks later.

"Ms. Romanowsky, you indicated here that you have smoked marijuana before. Is that correct?" the short sergeant asked.

"Yes, sir, that is correct."

"But it says here in your 2007 application that you have never smoked marijuana. Do you mean to tell me that you smoked marijuana *while* you were employed at the police department?"

"No sir, I have not smoked marijuana since I have worked here," I responded.

He looked at me quizzically. "If you didn't smoke it while you worked here, then are you telling me that you smoked it *before* you applied, and you lied on your initial application for employment?"

"Yes sir, that is correct."

"Why would you do that? What am I missing?" he shot back in an unconvinced tone.

"My dad told me to lie the first time, and so I did because I trusted him. But I have felt so much guilt about it that I knew I needed to come clean this time around, because it is the right thing to do. I smoked marijuana once, and never again."

"Your father, as in, Agent Romanowsky the parole officer?" He stared at me through narrowed eyes.

"Yes, that one."

"Why on earth should I believe you that your parole officer father told you to lie on an application to a law enforcement agency?"

"Well, he still wears his wedding ring and talks about his wife around the station, but he and my mom have been living separately for almost a year. So, clearly, he doesn't always live in reality," I quipped in a shaky voice. I felt a sense of immense relief for telling my truth, and instant regret and shame for revealing his.

"I'm sure you understand that we're going to have to ask your father about this."

"Yeah, go ahead—he will tell you the truth," I responded naively.

Two weeks later, the phone rang.

"We spoke to your dad—he said he never told you to lie on any application."

My stomach dropped to the floor. "But he did, I swear! You can even call my mom and ask her!"

Two minutes later, Mom's phone rang. I stood in the kitchen and watched as she spoke to the sergeant, her voice rising in anger.

"Yes, yes, I am familiar with the situation... She came to me with concerns about what to say, and I told her to talk to her dad. I thought he would encourage her to be honest about it—that everyone tries smoking marijuana and it's not a big deal! Instead, he fed her some cockamamie story about smoking crabgrass. I don't know why he did that—he's created a hell of a mess for no reason! He seems to have a tenuous relationship with the truth."

I got the promotion. Dad and I never discussed it again.

11

FRACTURES

It was a weekend in spring when mom and Launa came to visit me at my college apartment in Santa Barbara. We had plans to meet up with some girlfriends from high school and their moms for a mother-daughter dinner date.

Mom and Launa arrived at my apartment an hour before we were supposed to meet the others for dinner. Mom sat down on our squishy purple couch. Her already short frame sank even lower to the ground as the purple couch sucked her into its folds. I sat on the circular barstools in the kitchen opposite the couch, my tall thin frame awkwardly towering over Mom.

She looked up at me and told us that she and Dad were divorcing.

I wasn't exactly shocked. No, they didn't fight more than any other average couple when we were growing up, but they rarely acted like they were in love, either. Theirs seemed like a transactional relationship, a business partnership. They had been in the business of raising kids, and now that the kids were raised, the business was over, and the partnership was folding.

"Is there anything you want to know?"

"No."

"How do you feel?" she followed up.

"I don't know," I responded curtly. I hated when she asked me that.

"I don't know" was my go-to response for everything. Every time I said it, Mom grew more exasperated. "Why won't you just talk to me?" she had begged me when I was a child. But I couldn't talk to her because I never truly knew how I felt.

At age twenty, I was no different than I was at age six—I couldn't process the information that quickly and even if I *could* process it, I still didn't have the vocabulary to put my feelings into words.

Mom had just dropped an emotional bombshell on us, and neither of us knew what to say.

So, we did what we always did and carried on as though nothing out of the ordinary was happening.

In hindsight, it was probably more of a shock for me than it was for my sister. She was still living at home at the time and had a front-row seat to the downward spiral of my parents' marriage. She learned before I did about my dad staying out late at night and coming home to sleep on the couch. I took it for granted that I was living away at college and was able to immerse myself in my own life without worrying about what was going on at home.

Thirty awkward minutes later, the three of us drove to State Street to visit our friends for dinner. Sitting in the car with my mom and my sister gave me flashbacks to the time my sister and I drove home from the hospital after witnessing Uncle Nicoli die. We were physically close, but emotionally, we were all so far apart.

Two other sets of mothers and daughters waited for us at the hibachi restaurant—all four of them completely oblivious to the news we had just received.

That night, we swapped stories with our friends over fried rice and flaming onion towers and carried on as if it were any other dinner. But it wasn't. Inside, I felt so much shame. Shame that I was now even more different than them. Shame that my life, once again, had been struck by tragedy.

I was acutely aware that their mothers would go home to their fathers that night. Their mothers would go home and share with their fathers about their evening. They would laugh over the chef who flicked pieces of shrimp into the mouths of other diners. Then they would get into bed, their bodies huddled together in a safe and warm cocoon of blankets.

Meanwhile, my mom would go home to an empty house. I had no idea where my dad lived now.

These friends had grown up with me and knew my father—the external story he presented, at least. The external story he presented to the world was that he and my mother were happily married, raising two daughters—stellar students and athletes. Steady jobs, a beautiful home. Church-going folks. They had it all together... until they didn't.

I wasn't shocked that they were getting divorced, but I was ashamed. Why? It was 2008; divorce was hardly taboo. In fact, forty to fifty percent of all first marriages end in divorce, right? My parents were hardly unique. And yet, I didn't want them to be part of that statistic. I wanted to hold onto the external narrative. I wanted to keep it together. A divorce was one more loss, piled on top of a stack of losses that was precariously close to toppling over. Another mark against me, each tragedy taking me further and further away from my friends and their seemingly perfectly normal lives.

I turned further and further into myself.

I DON'T REMEMBER when Mom first told us about Dad's infidelity—or why she did, to be honest. But somehow, we learned. I shouldn't have been shocked, but I was. All those late nights he was gone weren't just spent tracking down parolees, apparently.

Although I learned about the infidelity almost immediately after I learned about the divorce, it was a full year later that I found out about the biggest betrayal—Rosie. A sweet name that left a bitter taste in my mouth for years to come.

Growing up, we spent a lot of time with Rosie, her spouse, and her kids, since they were part of our family. We spent the holidays together and went on vacation together. My sister and I spent weekends at Rosie's house, where we watched movies and ate ice cream and stayed up late with her kids.

And somewhere along the line, between the holiday weekends and the trips to Montana, Dad and Rosie began to have an affair. It's bad enough to be unfaithful to your wife. But to be unfaithful to your wife, by having an affair with a close family member? Well, that was just too much for me to comprehend.

By the time I learned about the affair, Rosie and her spouse had long since separated and so had my mom and dad. Both relationships were driven apart for different reasons. But even though the affair had occurred a decade earlier and was not the actual impetus for my parents' divorce, the revelation was still a bombshell. Learning that fact made my entire childhood feel like a farce. What else had been going on that I was unaware of? What other secrets did my parents keep? What other lives did my dad live?

I was so angry with Dad then—and ashamed. I didn't tell anybody what I had learned because I was too embarrassed. How could I possibly explain that my dad had an affair with someone else in my own family? So, I didn't—I stuffed it inside and tried to ignore it.

I continued to dive headfirst into my studies. If I just kept moving, I wouldn't crash.

Dad never talked to us about it—the separation or the infidelity.

In fact, the closest he ever got to discussing the separation was two years later, when he spontaneously muttered, "Sorry for messin' things up on the home front" before he hopped in his car and drove off, leaving us to wonder what had just happened.

Over the years, I had slowly begun to realize that my parents were not infallible. Like the time the Christmas tree fell over when I was ten and broke several beautiful ornaments. The falling tree didn't stun me as much as the moment I heard my mom yell, "Oh SHIT!" as the ornaments crashed onto the floor and shattered. I had never heard her use that word before.

But hearing Mom swear over the broken Christmas ornaments was nothing compared to learning about Dad's secret affair with Rosie. It wasn't just that he was a human capable of making mistakes. I was also learning that he was capable of deeply hurting *me*, his child. How could two grown adults with steady jobs, welcoming homes, beautiful spouses, and good children make such a catastrophically selfish decision? A decision that decimated family relationships and sent everyone into spirals of shame and confusion. How could a parent *do that* to their child?

I was so angry and disgusted with Dad, but I was also incapable of saying anything to him about it. I could barely sit through a kissing scene in a PG-13 movie with him without squirming with embarrassment and discomfort; how was I going to confront him about his R-rated life?

And so, I didn't say anything to him.

But the thing I learned, over and over again, is that no matter how deeply hurt I was by Dad's behaviors—at my very core, I still always loved him. And because I loved him, I wanted to protect him. Because I wanted to protect him, I didn't talk about his imperfections. And so, I held them in.

His secrets became mine.

THE YEARS after Mom and Dad separated were strange. Since Dad never wanted to talk to us about anything of substance, I had a lot of unanswered questions. Half the time, we didn't even know where he was. He moved apartments constantly, and we were never sure where he was living.

It bothered me that I didn't always know where he was living or what he was doing. When people asked me how he was, I never really knew how to answer. Those days, the most we saw Dad was when he would show up unannounced at work just to "check in" on us, or when he would invite us to dinner every few weeks. Dad would always go through cycles with his restaurants. I divide the years of memories by restaurant: the Mesa Café years, the California Pizza Kitchen years, the Brophy Bros. years.

It was September 2008, during the California Pizza Kitchen years, when Launa and I inadvertently found out that Dad was dating someone new. I had come home for the weekend from college, and we were hanging out in the kitchen. I sat in a tall barstool chair while Mom stood at the kitchen sink washing dishes. The small white tiles were cool against my cheek as I leaned my face against the counter.

Our kitchen window looked out at the front porch, so I saw Dad's imposing figure walking up to the door before I heard the knock—how strange for him to knock on the door of the house where he had lived for the last fifteen years.

Almost immediately after he walked inside, Mom started peppering him with questions about their credit card bill.

"How dare you charge these expensive dinners with your new girlfriend on *our* credit card," she spewed. "Did you really think I wouldn't see the bill, or did you not care?"

I left the kitchen and retreated to the room near the fireplace—out of the line of fire, but close enough to hear what was being said.

"What I do is none of your business anymore, remember?" Dad

retorted before he grabbed a stack of his mail and left without saying goodbye. Leaving as quickly as he had come.

I stormed back into the kitchen. "Why did you do that?" I yelled at Mom. "He was just coming to get his mail. You don't know who he went to dinner with! You asked him about a new girlfriend just to try to make us mad at him."

My voice shook with rage before I noticed that I had made her cry. Just as quickly as my rage had come, it left. Guilt immediately overtook me as my mom and I stood in the kitchen together, staring at each other and crying. Each of us crying for different reasons. I felt like a fool for yelling at her. Dad was the one who cheated on her—why was I blaming her? I should have been livid with Dad, but instead, I lashed out at her.

I was confused and didn't know how to make sense of everything that was happening with Dad. He was always my biggest champion—he never missed an opportunity to tell me how smart I was and how proud he was of me. If he thought I was so brilliant, how did he think he would get away with lying to me so much?

Two weeks after the kitchen fight, Launa and I met Dad for dinner at the CPK in El Paseo in Santa Barbara. I was just waiting for him to make the announcement to us. For him to confirm that he did have a new girlfriend. I didn't even care if he was dating—it wasn't like I held illusions of him and Mom getting back together. It wasn't the *girlfriend* that bothered me, it was the *lying* about it.

At dinner that night, Dad talked about the latest hike he had done and the latest arrest he had made. He asked us how we were doing at school, and then launched into another story about himself —always directing the narrative. I stared down at my plate as the ranch dressing dripped off my pizza. I couldn't bring myself to look him in the eye. At the end of dinner, Launa and I walked through El Paseo, lamenting to each other about how difficult these dinners were, and how frustrating it was that Dad could not be honest with us.

A few storefronts down, we stopped to look inside the shop. While I gazed at the brightly colored sweatpants with the word "PINK" plastered all over them, I noticed movement out of the corner of my eye. I turned around just in time to see Dad hop behind a kiosk to hide. He had been following us. Always keeping a watchful eye on us. I turned back toward the clothes, and he slunk away into the shadows, his footsteps softly echoing against the Spanish tiles.

COOCOO FOR COCO PUFFS

The holidays after the divorce were the hardest for me. Dad had never been a big holiday person. He didn't know how to give or accept gifts, and he always acted very awkward around presents. A product of his poor upbringing. Because the holidays were not important to him, he also never made plans with us.

Mom, quite the opposite, would start planning holidays six months in advance. I never wanted to commit to her because I was anxious and angry. I wanted to give Dad a chance to do something of his own, to make a big plan and surprise us. But that never happened. Often, he would wait until the last second and then tell us he had no plans. We'd feel sorry for him and then plan something ourselves.

The first year after the separation was the worst. Even as a young adult, being a child of divorced parents is hard to navigate. I remember that Thanksgiving vividly. Mom wanted us to take pictures in the backyard. I wanted to do anything but that. How could she want to take pictures of our "family" without Dad? It wasn't a family anymore. I didn't want a "family" picture without him. She wanted a new beginning—I was grasping for our old reality, even though I knew that image of the family we had was a facade.

That year, we had learned where Dad was living because of an ill-fated trip to the gas station. To show some financial support, Dad had given Launa a credit card that she could use for gas. She drove into the gas station and attempted to fill up her car. When the screen prompted her for the zip code of the card holder, she dutifully entered "93003"—the zip code where we had lived our entire lives. But that didn't work. She attempted "93004"—the second-closest zip code to our house—and still it didn't work.

DECLINED PLEASE REMOVE CARD.

DECLINED PLEASE REMOVE CARD.

DECLINED PLEASE REMOVE CARD.

The screen yelled at her. She was frustrated and ashamed. She had no gas, and—as she had just realized the hard way—she had no idea where her father was living.

A few weeks later, we learned. Dad invited us to check out his new apartment a few days after Thanksgiving. Begrudgingly, we accepted the offer.

We arrived at the apartment on the other side of town one evening and trudged up the exterior wooden stairs to the second-level entry. I was anticipating a bare apartment, a bachelor pad scraped together with secondhand furniture and no décor. I was shocked when we entered the apartment and were greeted with a warmly and nicely decorated place. *Perhaps it came fully furnished?* I thought.

I let myself believe that Dad had scored a fully furnished apartment. Until I needed to get a drink and wandered into the kitchen. As I reached for the handle of the refrigerator door, my breath caught and my arm stayed frozen in an outreached position. There, on the refrigerator, was a picture of Dad and another woman. Hugging and smiling into the camera.

So, Dad hadn't scored a fully furnished apartment. He was living with the new girlfriend he wouldn't tell us about.

I couldn't believe he didn't tell us that he was inviting us over to his girlfriend's place for Thanksgiving. And even more so, I couldn't believe that he (or maybe she?) was clueless enough to leave that picture on the refrigerator when we came over. A braver person might have snatched the picture off the refrigerator and marched back to the living room. That person might have waved the photo in the air while yelling, "When were you going to tell us about this, huh, huh??"

But I didn't do either of those things. I quickly poured my drink and walked back to the living room as if nothing had happened. Later, when Dad got up to use the bathroom, I leaned over and whispered to Launa to go check out the refrigerator. That was my way of alerting the troops that we were in foreign territory. Enemy soil.

The two of us gossiped angrily the whole way home. Can you believe that he did that? How could he invite us over to some woman's house without telling us that he is dating her? Speaking of her...who was she and *where* was she, anyway? Why wasn't she at dinner? For someone who does police work, how could he be so dumb and leave that picture up? Or maybe—I opined—maybe he did it on purpose and that was his way of telling us?

Looking back at everything that have happened over the decades, it is incredible how often I kept quiet about these monumental things that happened between me and Dad. There were so many opportunities to confront him on his stories, on his twists and turns and half-truths. But the reality is, I didn't want to. In hindsight, somewhere deep down, I think I knew that if I confronted him, it would not end well. We didn't have the tools for difficult discussions. If I ever let him know how deeply he had hurt me with his behaviors, it would have crushed him. I don't think he could have handled it emotionally. And so, I kept quiet and went along for the ride.

DURING ONE OF Dad's post-divorce unannounced visits to our house to pick up his mail, he announced abruptly, "I won't be getting my mail here anymore. I am moving to Lake Tahoe in thirty days."

"What? Lake Tahoe? What are you going to do there?" I retorted.

"I'll figure it out. I will work in a casino or something!"

Dad could hardly stand being indoors and hated cigarettes. What was he talking about, working in casino?

But there was no time for discussion. Under his breath, he made a strange comment about having no more living family and then as quickly as he came, he left.

LAKE TAHOE WAS the furthest he had ever been from us. Aside from not understanding why he moved there, I was irritated at how far away he chose to move. It wasn't like it was convenient for us to visit.

Two months after he moved, Launa and I set out to make the eight-hour trip to Tahoe to visit him. We drove in her new Honda Civic with a GPS map—a rarity in 2013. We spent hours in the car together, driving through the winding forests, listening to rap music until a detour led us to a dimly lit, unmarked road. We laughed nervously out of fear, as we imagined plunging to our deaths off a cliff in the aptly named "Shady Acres." Thankfully, we found our way through, and arrived at Dad's cabin around midnight. We should have realized that the detour along the unmarked path was a warning sign for what was to come that weekend.

The next morning started out pleasantly enough. Dad's new place was a comfortable, two-story three-bedroom cabin in Incline Village. The cabin was surrounded by stunning pine trees, their peaked tops stretching up to the sky. The sun reflected off the turquoise waters of Lake Tahoe in the distance.

But the beautiful day took a negative turn in the late afternoon.

Dad's cabin was across the alley from a brand-new grocery store, and we walked over to the shopping center to gather some ingredients for dinner. Launa had recently written a paper for her undergraduate English literature class about how growing up as a WASP had given her great benefits in this world, and she sometimes felt guilty about it. As we walked through the grocery store, she tried to explain how our whole family was privileged in America, simply because we were born white. Unfortunately, Dad didn't take kindly to this lesson. He immediately fired off at her in the middle of the grocery store about how foolish she was for feeling guilty for being a white woman in America, and how she had no idea how good she had it. He ranted and raved about growing up poor to immigrant parents, and how there was no way that he could be considered "privileged" given his poor upbringing and the pain he had to endure as a child.

There was nothing in my life more intimidating than Dad when he was angry. His voice grew louder, his words more clipped and his righteous anger could suck the air out of any room. His striking blue eyes, normally a spot of beauty, became cold and sharp—like a laser cutting through metal—sparks flying.

We grabbed our groceries and headed back to the cabin, Dad marching a few steps ahead of us with the two of us trailing sheepishly behind him. A cool evening breeze blew gently, causing goosebumps to appear on my forearms. As the breeze flowed through the pine trees, light brown pine nettles swirled around us—

the dead remnants of the old trees sluffed off to make room for new growth.

We made it back to the cabin and entered the dimly lit foyer. Although Dad had been living in the cabin for a few months, the damp musty smell of an unoccupied space still lingered in the air. The furnishings were cold and uninviting—ghosts of the person who lived there before Dad.

We went to the kitchen and the sound of rustling plastic filled the air as we unloaded the groceries in silence. The silence was shattered as the *POP* of a cork sliding out of a wine bottle punctured the air. Dad poured himself a glass of chardonnay—fuel for the continuing argument.

My fight-or-flight instincts kicked in and I quickly left the room, retreating to the small study down the hall. I had no desire to fight with Dad—not then, and not ever. But Launa didn't give up as easily as I did.

A few minutes later, Dad and Launa picked up where they had left off in the grocery store.

"*You* try being a child named Boris during the Cold War and then tell me again how I was so privileged!" Dad bellowed.

I could hear the exasperation in Launa's voice as she challenged Dad on his limited view of "privilege." She tried to tell him that "white privilege" didn't mean that he had a great childhood; it meant that he wasn't discriminated against *because* of his race and that his whiteness afforded him a very basic advantage over his non-white counterparts.

But there was no convincing Dad. Launa and Dad spent the next hour yelling at each other in the kitchen—arguing over white privilege and our role as white people in society. Meanwhile, I hid from the blowout in the study. I curled up on the armchair, tucking my legs underneath me and letting the squishy pillows envelope me as I tried to hide from the escalating fight.

Part of me felt guilty for not coming to my little sister's aid and for leaving her to fend for herself against Dad's anger. I agreed with what she was saying. But the other part of me was puzzled by her choice to argue with Dad. Didn't she know she would never win an argument with him this way? Why did she voluntarily subject herself to such anger and vitriol?

As Dad poured himself glass after glass of chardonnay, his arguments didn't become better, he simply got louder. He raged at my sister—calling her ungrateful for the life he had worked so hard to give her, for the privileges he wanted so badly to enjoy when he was a child but couldn't.

Launa sobbed as Dad flung his negative energy at her like a spear—piercing her exterior. Eventually, she stormed off, leaving Dad and his wine alone in the kitchen.

"Thanks for nothing," she spat once she found me. By then, I had slunk away to the bedroom to curl up under the covers.

"I just don't understand why you fight with him. You know he will never change..." I responded meekly.

"Because he's *wrong*," she said. With that, she slipped into her pajamas and rolled to her side; the sound of her sniffles put us both to sleep.

THE NEXT EVENING, Dad tried to act as if nothing had happened. He insisted we all go to dinner at a restaurant and sit outside to enjoy the lake.

As we waited for our food, once again, Dad drank glass after glass of chardonnay. It was a warm summer evening, but he was wearing a long-sleeved shirt. After he drank a few glasses of wine, he rolled up his sleeve and pointed to a circular brown spot on his forearm. As a kid, I always thought Dad's arms had freckles from the sun. In that moment, it suddenly became clear to me that freckles don't appear in such perfectly symmetrical circles.

Dad's eyes welled with tears as he spontaneously began to tell us the story of how he received the circular scars. When Dad was a young boy, his father told him that if he could get a cigarette to burn through a dollar bill, he could keep the dollar bill. My dad, never wanting to appear weak, and needing the money, agreed to the challenge. My grandfather wrapped the bill tightly around my dad's forearm and held the lit cigarette against it. The cigarette smoldered and burned my father's arm, but he bit his tongue and refused to scream. He did this for several minutes, until the flesh under the dollar bill began to smoke and he writhed in pain. My grandfather snatched back the dollar and exposed my father's forearm, the freshly charred skin still smoldering. The dollar bill was still fully intact. My Dad was left with a burned forearm and no dollar—the victim of a cruel Russian bar trick.

"What kind of man would burn his own son with a cigarette as a joke? You call that white privilege?" Dad whispered to me and Launa as the waitress set our food down on the table. A tear fell from his eye, and inside, my heart broke. My sister stared off into the distance.

"My father was a very, very bad man," he muttered.

None of us spoke again during the rest of the meal.

THE NEXT MORNING, we packed the car and prepared to make the long drive back home. As we got in Launa's Civic and prepared to leave, Dad placed his large hand on the top of the car and bent over to look inside at us both.

"Have a safe drive home, girls. And uhm, I guess I went a little 'Coo Coo for Coco Puffs' the other night..."

He closed the door before we could respond, tapped on the roof twice, and began to walk back into the house.

That was the closest thing to an apology we ever heard from Dad.

Launa and I erupted with laughter. Then we backed out of the driveway and headed South. Just keep moving, and you won't feel a thing.

As we drove home, I thought about what Dad had said about his father burning him. I thought about what my mom had told me years before about my grandfather abusing children—physically, emotionally, sexually. Had my grandfather molested my father? The thought sickened me and cut me to my core. I felt profound sadness for my father—for whatever he had experienced as a child. I was grateful that he had shielded us from the traumas for so long, and I longed to comfort him. To tell him it wasn't his fault.

Almost as quickly as Dad had moved to Tahoe, he was back in Ventura. To celebrate his return to town, he wanted to meet us for dinner at Abuela's Mexican restaurant. There was an Abuela's right down the street from our house in Ventura, but he insisted we meet him at the one in Oxnard.

"I'm already here, but you can come whenever you're ready. When you come, just go ahead and pay the valet to park," he instructed.

Valet? Abuela's was a casual restaurant, not fine dining. Since when did they need a valet? We found out soon enough.

We arrived and found Dad sitting at the bar in the middle of the restaurant. He saw us immediately as we walked in, since he always sat facing the front door wherever we went. He hopped off the barstool and quickly strode over to us, his long legs propelling him across the floor in four short steps. As he walked, his black dress shirt billowed behind him. He reached up with his tan hand and swept four fingers across his forehead, brushing his brown hair out of his eyes.

"Hey, girls," he greeted us with his usual awkward half-hug. "So, did you park in the valet? I picked up a new PI gig."

We looked at him in surprise.

"Yeah," he continued, "ever since the fitness center was built in this little strip mall, the lot is full of yahoo gangbangers fresh out of prison trying to get buff for their girlfriends. They just come to this gym and clog up the parking lot for hours. Now Abuela's is losing business because their patrons can't get parking. So, they pay me just to sit inside and count how many cars come in during rush hour and how many go to 24 Hour Fitness versus Abuelas. I think they're gonna sue the gym. Can you believe it? They just pay me to count people!"

I wondered if they paid for the beers he drank too.

"Boris, your table for five is ready!" the pretty hostess called out, as she stacked five sticky menus in her hand.

Five? There were only three of us. My sister and I exchanged a confused side glance.

We sat at a big wooden table toward the front of the restaurant, so Dad could still see out the front window and continue counting cars.

We got settled into our seats, and Launa and I glanced over the menus. As Dad looked out the window, he furrowed his brow, hopped up out of his seat and walked toward the door.

I craned my neck as much as I could without creating a scene, and that's when I saw them—a short woman with long blonde hair and a young child in tow. My mind quickly flashed back to the photograph on the refrigerator in the unfamiliar apartment.

Two more patrons of Abuelas who had a hard time finding

parking. And that was how we met Dad's girlfriend and her son for the first time.

Their unexpected arrival at the restaurant was so shocking to me that I don't remember anything else about the dinner. Did he tell us that she was a hair stylist at that first meeting, or did we learn that later? Did her son tell us about his baseball team then, or did he just sit in silence? The details don't really matter to me anymore. Only the feelings remain.

———

SIX MONTHS after I graduated from UCSB, I moved back to Ventura and rented my first apartment together with Rob.

The two story, two-bedroom apartment felt like a palace after living in cramped quarters with three other girls for the previous four years.

In April 2010, Rob and I sat together in our spare room (we had a *spare* room!) to do our taxes. We both were fortunate enough to get jobs right after getting our degrees. Filing our own tax returns in our own apartment was momentous—we felt like true adults.

"I finished mine this morning. I'm going to get a $2,500 refund!" Rob exclaimed, mesmerized by the amount of money.

"I can't wait to see how much I get back. Maybe we can use it to go on a vacation!" I responded.

I sat down at the small desk, pulled out my W2 and opened my laptop. Rob sat behind me and walked me through the prompts of TurboTax, making sure I answered all the questions correctly.

I hit "COMPLETE" and I held my breath while the program worked its magic to spit out the calculations of my new fortune.

Thank you for using Turbo Tax. Based on our calculations, you are entitled to a refund in the amount of $0.00 dollars. Please check the next button to proceed with signing your return.

Zero dollars?

"Whaaaaaaat?" Rob yelled. "That makes no sense—we made the same amount of money, and I am getting $2,500 back!"

The visions of a grand vacation vanished as quickly as they had come.

"I don't understand," I muttered. "I must have entered something wrong on one of the pages." Instantly, I assumed I was the problem.

As it turned out, I had done nothing wrong. Through a series of phone calls, I learned that my dad had claimed me as a dependent on his taxes so he would get a break on his *own* taxes. According to the IRS, a parent could claim an adult child as a dependent if the parent provided the child with more than half of their total support for the year, and the child couldn't claim themselves. Claiming a child as a deduction could save a taxpayer approximately $4,050 in income taxes.

At that time in my life, I was working two separate part-time jobs and going to night school. I was proud of myself for finishing college and getting a job so I could move into my own apartment. Dad was not financially supporting me at all.

I was furious. It's not that I wanted my dad to pay extra in taxes, or that I was ungrateful for anything he *had* provided me thus far—but it was the way he went about it. He singlehandedly made a decision that would benefit *him*, to my detriment. He didn't talk to me about it or tell me he was going to do it. In fact, if it weren't for Rob, I probably wouldn't have ever even thought to question the fact that I wasn't getting a refund.

I was fired up, and I called Dad and confronted him about it. "Did you claim me as a dependent on your taxes?" I said flatly, barely hiding my resentment.

"Oh yeah, Boomer, that will save me about $4,050 in income taxes! It's expensive being divorced, you know...your mom got the house and I have all these bills to pay..."

I hated when he brought up the divorce. Always complaining that Mom got the house, as if she wasn't worthy. As if the divorce came out of left field and he had no part in their downfall.

"Well, I am NOT your dependent. I pay for everything myself and I am entitled to a refund! I called your CPA and told him that he better change your return, so I get my refund."

"Wait a minute, that's going to cost me $4,050!"

I hung up without answering.

A bolt of electricity pulsed through my body. I rarely, if ever, confronted Dad. I couldn't believe what I had just done. I was so proud of myself for speaking my truth and calling him out.

However, that pride was short-lived. As soon as the initial adrenaline of the moment wore off, I felt intense guilt and shame.

How ungrateful was I, to yell at my dad over $2,500? After all he had given me in my life, I couldn't believe how angry I was over the stupid tax refund.

I felt immense sadness for him and for the situation he must have been in – how much *did* he need that extra tax break?

In addition to feeling sad, I felt confused. He wouldn't do something to intentionally take money from his own daughter, right? Maybe he just didn't understand the question on the tax form? Maybe he didn't realize that by claiming me as his dependent, he was taking away my right to get a refund?

Maybe I should call the CPA back and tell him I had made a mistake. Maybe I should do this to help Dad out. After all, that's what family does, right? Help each other out?

The thoughts swirled around in my brain like mini cyclones of confusion. I knew Dad loved me. I knew Dad was proud of me. I knew Dad would drop anything to help me if I needed it. How then, could this same Dad do something that would harm me? Was he naïve? Selfish? Both?

13

LAW SCHOOL AND ICU

After college, I turned my eyes toward law school. I was still working at the Santa Barbara Police Department and was also participating in an internship at the District Attorney's office. I spent my days examining evidence in the police property room and my afternoons arranging exhibits for murder trials. Naturally, given my background and my dad's job, I had a desire to become a District Attorney to be a voice for the victims of violent crimes.

Because I wanted to stay in Ventura or Santa Barbara County and work as a District Attorney, I decided to stay local and go to the Ventura College of Law at night. Going to the VCL would allow me to continue to work while putting myself through school, without incurring too much debt. I was afraid that if I went away to a bigger law school, I literally would not be able to afford to move back to our small town and become a District Attorney.

I started at the VCL in fall of 2010. The schedule was rigorous. I would wake up at 5:30 a.m. and drive to the bus stop, where I would hop on the city bus traveling to Santa Barbara. I'd put in a full day of work in Santa Barbara, before heading back to Ventura on the bus. From there, I'd grab my car and drive to school, where I'd go to class from 6:30-9:30 p.m. three nights a week. On the nights I didn't have class, I'd lock myself in my room and study for hours at a time.

I was living with Rob, but I wasn't really living. I was consumed by my schoolwork and the desire to succeed in law school. I was terrified of failing. I read, briefed cases, and read some more. My family refers to those years as "the missing years" because people rarely saw me. My singular focus was succeeding in school.

AT 6 A.M. on January 11, 2011, my phone rang. No good news ever comes at 6 a.m.

I rolled over to grab my phone and my anxiety skyrocketed when I noticed who was calling—Dad's newest girlfriend, Lori.

Lori and Dad had traveled to Northern California to go skiing. The night before, he mentioned to her that he had a dull pain in his abdomen that would not subside. As the night went on, the pain became excruciating, and Lori had to rush Dad to the hospital. After hours in the Emergency Room, the doctors finally determined that he had an unknown blockage in his colon. Due to the dangers of the unknown blockage, they would need to perform emergency exploratory surgery. The surgery was scheduled for that evening at 6:30 p.m.—the same exact time as my contracts class.

I went to class that evening and approached my new professor. I told him that I knew cell phones were not allowed in class, but that I would need to keep mine on my desk that night because my dad was having emergency exploratory surgery and I needed to be able to answer if the doctor called.

The professor looked at me incredulously. "Why are you even here? You can go home!"

I assured him there was no need for me to leave—the hospital Dad was in was hours away. Plus, it was only the second week of class, and I didn't want to fall behind.

My phone buzzed an hour later, and I stepped outside the classroom to take the call. My heart was pounding as I swiped to answer.

During the surgery, the doctors discovered that Dad's colon had been perforated during his 2005 surgery. Over the last five-and-a-half years, the colon had slowly twisted. Like a snake suffocating its prey, the colon had wrapped around itself, constricting tighter and tighter, until a portion of it rotted and died. When that happened, a complete blockage occurred, leaving Dad in a life-threatening situation.

Normally, the doctors would simply remove the damaged part. However, because a significant portion of Dad's colon had already been removed during the botched surgery in 2005, the doctors had no choice but to remove his entire colon.

Four days after Dad was admitted to the hospital, I received a picture via email from him. In the picture, he is standing outside of the hospital directly in front of the red EMERGENCY sign. A snowcapped Mount Shasta fills the background. Dad's army-green hiking pants and brown boots peek out from beneath his light-blue hospital gown. With one hand, he holds onto an IV pole, two plastic bags filled with fluids, their plastic cords running to his body. The gastric tube and catheter are still in place. With the other hand, he holds a green sign: "Caution, Slippery Surface."

That picture is how he told us all he was going to be okay.

Dad was in ICU for four days. I went to work and school every one of those days, and never missed a night of reading or an assignment.

Just keep moving, and you won't crash.

Dad outside the hospital.

A FEW MONTHS LATER, I strolled through the beer aisle of Vons grocery store. The fluorescent lights illuminated my tired eyes as I ran through my options.

It was a Thursday evening and I had just finished work as a paralegal. It wasn't a bad day at work, just a long one—and hell, I just wanted a beer. This scene was totally atypical. I could not remember the last time I had cracked a beer open on a Thursday night. But this day was different, for some reason.

Six-pack? No, that's too much. I grabbed a 40oz Blue Moon instead. Although in retrospect, a six-pack would have been more bang for my buck. I grabbed the bottle and turned to head to the checkout and there he was.

He was thinner than normal—still recovering from the time he'd spent in ICU that past January. Yet somehow, he was still muscular. His brown hair that normally hung over his forehead was forced upwards unnaturally, the result of a new hairstyle. Streaks of gray were starting to form near his temples. *When did that happen? I wondered.*

To the casual eye, he was wearing black pants and a jean button-up shirt, but I knew underneath was his State Parole shirt, handcuffs, and his gun. An awkward hug confirmed he was also wearing his bulletproof vest. But underneath all that armor stood a shell. When I was a child, he was a man who represented everything that was strong and powerful—brave and fearless and different than all the other dads. Now, as I stood there in the store with my 40oz of Blue Moon in hand, I knew that the bulletproof vest wasn't the only thing between us.

The vest was a guard against bullets, but even bulletproof vests aren't flawless—get shot in the side and you go down like a felled tree. It was there, in the middle of the store next to the new display of assorted olives that his cracked foundation became more evident than ever before.

"Well, I think Lori and I just aren't gonna make it," he blurted out after our hug and a simple salutation. He mumbled something under his breath about being bad at relationships—something he didn't need to tell me twice.

As his huge blue eyes welled, the whites becoming increasingly red, I couldn't help but feel sorry for him. Not only for his breakup, but for his complete loss of self. The surgery had taken out his colon; the breakup took a piece of his heart.

It was comical really—being stuck in the store with my dad telling me about his failed relationship. He always chose the worst times. Things that are best discussed in soft voices in the privacy of a home were blurted out in public spaces. Like the time a year earlier, when my sister and I were running to our car in the pouring rain and he chose that moment to say, "Oh, by the way, I broke my lease and moved in with Lori!" It was impossible for us to discuss it, as the rain poured down, and so all we could do was slam the car doors shut and laugh.

I should have been used to it by then, but I wasn't. Our relationship was comprised of nothing more than short, impersonal banter. And while I couldn't help but feel terrible for how his life was panning out—the other half of me couldn't shake the feeling that he did it to himself.

FOUR MONTHS after Dad's emergency surgery, I finished my first-year law school exams. After the exams, my study partners and I waited weeks for our professors to post our grades. Our professors had repeatedly warned us about the high fail rate of first-year law students, and how difficult it was to succeed. With each day that passed, my stomach grew tighter, and my anxiety kicked into high gear. *If I failed, what would I do then? How would I tell everyone that I had failed out of law school? What would I tell my family? My boss?*

Finally, one evening I received the email with my grades. I sat for a solid five minutes just staring at my glowing laptop screen before I finally pulled together the strength to open the email and learn my fate.

Congratulations! You have received the following grades: Constitutional Law: A; Torts: A; Contracts: A. Your class ranking is: 1/40.

I stared at the email in shock. Not only had I not failed—I had been wildly successful. My group chat started to blow up as my three closest study partners received their grades. Thankfully, they had all passed also. I let them know that I had passed, but I said nothing about my grades or my class rank. I was embarrassed and didn't know how to share my successes. I did not want to make anybody else feel less-than. But perhaps more importantly, I didn't really believe it myself. I thought perhaps there had been a mistake. I was a good student, yes, but the number one student in my law school class? Surely, I wasn't that smart.

I waited several days before I confided to my study partners that I had received the top grades. I sent them the following email with the subject line: "Confession."

> I must admit that after class tonight I felt kind of weird, like I was being vague and evasive whenever you guys talked about grades. And I wanted to tell you all in class, but I didn't want to be braggy or snotty or anything. And I basically didn't know what to say, but you're bound to find out sooner or later so I will just tell you... My class standing is #1 right now. And I am convinced it is because of my awesome study group.

Something that should have been a cause for celebration instead caused me to feel immense guilt. I wanted everyone else to be as successful as I was. At the same time, imposter syndrome wracked my body—I didn't believe I was a success, and I was afraid I would be exposed as a fraud.

It was a vicious cycle. Because I believed I would be exposed as a fraud, instead of slowing down, I *increased* the amount of time I put into studying. The first year must have been a fluke. Now, not only was I afraid of failing, but I was afraid of a very public failing—when everyone would soon realize that I wasn't as smart as they thought I was. I spent every evening and every weekend reading and studying.

The next two-and-a-half years of law school were the same—I worried obsessively about failing. I allowed myself little-to-no free time for pleasure and focused only on studying. Time after time, the grades came out and I received the top grade in every class. The end of the year celebrations were always extremely uncomfortable for me; I stood in front of my classmates and collected award after award. I received piles of certificates for getting the highest grade in every class. My friends and classmates supported me and cheered me on, but inside I still felt guilty and embarrassed. Who was I to receive these accolades and awards?

With every success, my anxiety grew and grew. The little girl who used to check her backpack every night was now a young adult who checked her computer notes every night instead. I was constantly on edge. I couldn't enjoy myself because I was always worried about my studies—any downtime was time that I should have been studying. I always told myself I'd have more fun when I graduated, once I took the bar exam, once I became a lawyer. Now was the time for focus—I could have fun later.

At least, that was the lie I told myself.

14

CHANGING NAMES

"It was a calm, still night in that small town. Everyone was tucked in bed, but in the shadows, lurked something a little more sinister..."

It was Friday night and Rob and I sat together on our small purple couch, engaged in our weekly ritual of snacking on Goldfish crackers and watching Dateline.

According to the quick introduction, this episode was about a "seemingly perfect marriage gone terribly wrong." We couldn't get enough Lester Holt and Keith Morrison.

At the commercial break, I went to our small kitchen to grab more Goldfish crackers. I felt slightly more sophisticated eating the parmesan flavored ones.

As I turned back to the living room, Rob awkwardly rolled off the couch and onto the floor. "Are you okay?"

"I'm sorry—I just can't wait any longer," he blurted out as he reached into his pocket.

Wait, is he on one knee?

"This is killing me. Will you marry me?!" He looked up at me with pleading eyes. Behind him, Keith Morrison returned to the screen.

Is my boyfriend proposing to me during an episode of Dateline about people who murdered their spouses?

Yes, yes he is.

"I'm sorry! I wanted to take you to the top of that big sand hill in Malibu and propose during sunset because you said once how romantic that would be. But, it's supposed to rain this weekend and I just cannot keep carrying this ring around!" Rob finished.

I burst into laughter.

"Yes!" I responded enthusiastically, as I kneeled to hug him and he slipped the ring onto my finger. Then we went back to the kitchen where I poured a celebratory coffee cup of red wine– we weren't fancy enough yet to own actual wine glasses.

I WAS NOT one of those women who had planned her ideal wedding since I was a little girl. Yet when it came time to plan, I had no trouble making decisions about how I wanted the day to look. I quickly picked out a location, a photographer, a menu and a wedding color scheme.

The hardest thing for me to plan was the father-daughter dance.

Despite everything that had happened with Dad over the last few years, I still loved him and wanted him to walk me down the aisle. But when the DJ asked me what song I wanted to use for a dance with my dad, I was stumped. First, I could not recall ever seeing my father dance. And now he and I were supposed to dance together? In public? But even more confusing to me was what song we would use for the dance.

We didn't have "a song" that was special to us. The only music that reminded me of Dad was the little jingle that would play on the local AM radio station when dad was driving and listening for traffic updates.

I spent weeks listening to music and reviewing songs online.

None of the traditional father-daughter dance songs felt right. Too sappy. Too corny. Too... not us.

Finally, one night I stumbled upon a suggestion on Reddit while searching for: "Beautiful but not corny songs for father-daughter dance when you love him but aren't emotionally close." Yes, there really are threads for these types of questions.

And it was there that I found it. The perfect song.

It was a warm summer night in August—an ideal night for an outdoor wedding. Elaborate centerpieces with purple roses, white baby's breath, and dangling crystals littered the circular tables. Family and friends milled about. String lights crisscrossed through the trees overheard, casting a warm glow over the dance floor that had been set up in the middle of the garden.

At the announcement of the DJ, I met my dad in the center of the dance floor and joined together to dance in front of one hundred and fifty friends, relatives, and a few strangers.

Natalie Merchant's soulful voice boomed from the speakers, and my heart felt full as I heard the opening lines about kindness and generosity.

Meanwhile, just like he would do at the movie theaters, Dad attempted to carry on a normal conversation with me at full volume while we tried not to step on each other with our two (four?) left feet.

"Well Boomer, you did a really good job here with this wedding planning!"

I smiled.

"I mean, the food is pretty good too! That's a lot of people to feed, and you got it done!"

I could feel the eyes of every wedding guest staring at us while we danced.

"You know, this is a really big deal. This whole wedding deal. You did a good job planning!"

"Thanks, Dad. I don't think we're supposed to talk about the menu when all these people are watching us dance though!"

Dad looked handsome that day, in his pressed gray tux with the deep purple napkin tucked into his breast pocket. But more importantly, he looked happy. Something I don't remember seeing in him in a long time. As the song ended, he brushed a happy tear from his eye and sniffed loudly, mumbling about hay fever as he exited the dance floor.

Smiling at Dad talking at full volume during the first dance.
Photo by Amanda Driver.

A YEAR AFTER OUR WEDDING, I finished law school as the number one student in my class. I spent the next three months studying for the bar upwards of ten hours a day. All of my hard work, all of those sleepless nights and countless hours of studying paid off. I passed the bar and was sworn in as an attorney in June 2014.

I had done it! I had succeeded! I had excelled at school and had all the accolades to show for it. I could finally relax. Or so I thought.

Three months later, I had the most debilitating anxiety attack of my life.

15

WHAT RELAXATION?

A normal Wednesday afternoon driving home from my new job as an attorney. I drove north on the 101 freeway. A road I have driven thousands of times in my life. Eminem and Rhianna blasted through the speakers as I whizzed past the familiar exits. Del Norte. Rice. Rose. Each exit bringing me closer to home where my new husband would be waiting for me.

As I attempted to keep up with Eminem's fast paced lyrics about being crazy, I wondered if the other drivers would expect me, in my pencil skirt and pearls, to be listening to this song? I smirked as I thought about it.

But as I drove closer to my exit, I noticed a familiar creeping feeling rising in my chest. It was that same creeping feeling I would get as a little girl, right before I would dash out of my room to check my backpack one more time. The same creeping feeling I would get before a law school exam, while we all waited for the professor to yell "BEGIN" so we could hurriedly flip over our papers to reveal the questions for the night. That same creeping feeling I would get before I saw the question and then began to aggressively type on my keyboard.

Except this time was different. There was no backpack to check.

No paper to type. No exam to flip over. There was nothing to quell the rising tide of my panic.

It bubbled up through my chest, expanding rapidly like lava flowing over the scorched earth around it, creating rivers of fire that burn up everything in their path.

Suddenly I felt the air escaping my lungs. It was as though I was being held underwater, being tossed by the waves, waiting for that moment when I would emerge from beneath and make a gulping gasp of air. Hungry for oxygen.

My hands trembled as I tried to guide the car toward home. Toward safety. As I gripped the steering wheel, I imagined myself veering off the road and smashing into the guard rail, my car spinning into a crunching heap of metal. How easily I could make that a reality by one slight twitch of my hand on the steering wheel. One wrong move, and everything would go up in flames. I was not suicidal by any stretch of the imagination, I did not *want* to twitch the wheel to cause the collision, but the fact that I had the ability to do so—that I could change my life so drastically in an instant—was extremely unnerving. The thoughts raced through my mind like cars whizzing around a race car track. *Whoosh. Whoosh. Whoosh.*

I tried to breathe through the panic, but no relief came. Eventually, I pulled over to the side of the road. I opened my phone and immediately searched psychologytoday.com for local therapists. I searched "anxiety" and "panic attacks" and pulled up the first results I could find. I sent all of them emails requesting to be seen "as soon as possible."

Two weeks later, I was in Roxanne's office. I was crying and telling her how great my life was. I didn't understand why I was having panic attacks. I had finished law school as the top student in my class. I had graduated with honors. I had passed the bar on my first try. I had recently gotten married and was living in a beautiful condo with my new husband. What on earth did I have to be panicking about?

It was then that Roxanne mentioned she had looked at my intake sheet. The one where I listed all the "major life events" that had happened to me in the last few years. My list was so long that I had to use the backside of the page. A collection of catastrophes. A table of contents of tragedies.

She thought that list might be a good place to start. But I didn't understand. Those things happened years ago. I had achieved so much since then. I had overcome those events. I had moved through them already. Why did we have to talk about them *now*?

But the truth was that I never really dealt with any of them. I just continued to work and achieve and push myself. I learned later that this was my way of coping. I used my achievements to mask my pain. If I just kept moving and accomplishing, I would never have to stop and fully feel my emotions.

So, when Roxanne began to ask me how I *felt* about things, I gave her my standard answer: "I don't know."

How did I feel about witnessing my uncle Nicoli die? How did I feel about my dad's cancer diagnosis and surgery? How did I feel about my parents getting divorced? How did I feel about learning my dad had affairs?

The truth was, I didn't know how I felt about any of it, because I never stopped long enough to think about it. Because I never stopped, I never processed. Because I never processed, I never felt things. I quickly learned from Roxanne that the body does not forget. My body remembered the pain and the trauma even if I tried to forget it. No amount of achievement was going to eradicate the pain that was sitting somewhere deep in my body, slowly pushing its way up.

It wasn't until I stopped moving for the first time in my life that the pain hit me like a freight train. Rendering me confused and completely debilitated.

AFTER THAT INITIAL MEETING, I began to sneak away to meet with Roxanne every other week. I simultaneously looked forward to our meetings and dreaded them. I didn't understand why we needed to discuss things that had happened so long ago. I hated it when she asked me how I felt about things, because I still didn't really know.

Like most therapists, she eventually got around to asking me about my childhood, the family dynamics and of course, my parents. Internally, I rolled my eyes. Did they teach this in How to Be a Therapist 101? I didn't see the point in talking about my parents, but I went along with it.

At some point, we got to talking about my dad. I told her about his cancer, about the divorce, and about the uptick in his drinking since the divorce. I told her how I began to ignore calls from him after a certain time of day, because they were too hard to handle. He wouldn't say anything mean, but he would ramble, and it was clear to me that he was intoxicated. I didn't like it, so I'd just ignore his calls until I could call him back the next morning.

I mentioned it as an aside. I didn't intend for it to be the main focus of therapy. We were supposed to be talking about my anxiety.

But oh, how wrong I was.

Roxanne immediately began to shift the focus of our meetings to my dad and his drinking. I didn't understand. *His drinking doesn't affect me*, I thought. He was never physically violent, he was never emotionally abusive, he always showed up for us as kids, coached our sports teams, took us on adventures and supported us. Sure, he made some terrible decisions, had some extramarital affairs, often told half-truths, and bounced from relationship to relationship, but that was *his* problem, not mine. Right?

But it was there, in Roxanne's office, that I began to really learn about alcoholism and the effect it has on the entire family. She showed me a list of questions to determine whether I had been affected by his drinking. Reading the list was like reading an autobiography.

1. Do you constantly seek approval and affirmation? (√)
2. Do you fail to recognize your accomplishments? (√)
3. Do you fear criticism? (√)
4. Do you overextend yourself? (√)
5. Have you had problems with your own compulsive behavior? (√)*

Turns out, it didn't matter that my dad was never drunk around me growing up. It didn't matter that he was high-functioning and in great physical shape, that he constantly supported me and he took us on great adventures. The effects of his drinking were pervasive, and they went deep. The way we didn't ever talk about our feelings. The way we soldiered on, after each catastrophe, never stopping to discuss what happened. The way we prioritized activity over rest, achievements over emotions. The way we kept secrets. The way we all tried to control everything. The disease of alcoholism touched everything that I knew as "normal."

After a while, Roxanne suggested I start going to a support group, because it might be helpful to connect with other people who had been affected by alcoholism.

That sounded like my worst nightmare. It was one thing to work on revealing my emotions to a therapist, in a safe little room on a safe little couch. It was quite another to expect me to go to big rooms and talk to *other* people about my problems. *Hell to the no*, I thought.

But, after Roxanne's constant nudging, I finally found the courage to try out the support group for families of alcoholics. And I am so glad I did, because those support group sessions changed my life. All my life, I had held in my struggles with anxiety. I kept my emotions to myself because I didn't want to burden other people with them. I didn't want to feel "less than" or different.

---

* *Did You Grow Up with a Problem Drinker* (S-25), copyright Al-Anon Family Group Headquarters, Inc., 1984. Permission granted.

But there, in those rooms, I was not alone. I heard from other people who had been raised by alcoholics and how it had affected them. I heard countless men and women share about their anxieties, their inability to process their emotions and their constant struggles to achieve. I was not alone. The liberation I felt was unbelievable.

It was there, in those rooms, that I started to understand the menacing sides of my father a bit more. Those erratic mood swings? The half-truths and flat out lies? The infidelities? The inability to connect emotionally? His traumas and the disease of alcoholism was the root of most of them. Did that excuse his behavior? Of course not. But it sure helped me to understand it.

My dad experienced a significant amount of trauma in his lifetime. As a child, he grew up in a violent household, the middle child of ten. They were poor. They were neglected and abused. There was no time for discussing feelings—he was fighting his siblings for scraps of food. His father was burning him with cigarettes, and worse.

When Dad was in high school, one of his classmates was brutally murdered by another classmate. I believe that this crime, and other incidents he witnessed, are what inspired him to go into law enforcement. As an adult, Dad dedicated his entire life to law enforcement, supervising high-risk sex offenders and murderers.

As a child, I revered him for the work he did. In my child's mind, he was stopping crime and keeping us safe. As an adult, I realized the toll that took on him. He didn't know how to escape the violence, and so he kept re-exposing himself to the horrors. He was obsessive about stopping crimes, protecting women and children, and keeping high-risk parolees off the streets.

The criminal justice system is deeply flawed, but there's no doubt that the work my dad did, the crime scenes he processed, and the victims he spoke to were real. He saw himself as their savior, and sometimes he was. He was always to first to jump into a difficult situation and help. He thrived on the chaos. He knew how to handle the chaos. It was the downtime he couldn't handle. It was the downtime he tried to avoid. The only coping skills he had were to exercise and to drink. And so, he stuffed his feelings and soldiered on. But the trauma was always right below the surface.

As a child, I didn't know any of this. But I still had an underlying sense of unease. I didn't have a rough upbringing. My parents did everything in their power to ensure that my sister and I had "normal" suburban childhoods. I had adventures, I had a safe and clean home, I was supported by my family, I excelled in school and sports. But we didn't discuss hard things.

My hyper-focus on perfectionism and control were distractions from the emotions swirling around inside of me that I didn't know how to process. Over time, as I went to more and more therapy sessions, my heart began to soften, and my anxieties began to lessen. I had spent so many years trying to gain control of my education and of my life—but that control was an illusion.

Once I began to learn about my own behaviors, I began to appreciate Dad's as well. Where I was focused on school, he was hyper-focused on his physical fitness. All those grueling hikes he took us on weren't just to show us the world—they were for him to emotionally check out. He had no other coping mechanisms other than exercising and then later, drinking.

Dad white-knuckled it through our childhood. I rarely saw him have more than a beer or two, or a glass of wine in my childhood. It was during my college years, after the divorce, that Dad's drinking got bad. There were times he would call and ramble on about nonsensical things. Late-night emails full of misspellings. Stories that didn't add up. Chunks of time missing. It was painful to watch. But in addition to being painful, sometimes it was rage-inducing.

Although I learned more about alcoholism and its effects on the family, I didn't really understand how to deal with it yet. I had compassion for Dad's pain, and I felt a new sense of understanding about how it affected me, but I also became resentful. Why couldn't he just get it together?

16

ANTI-HERO

Though Dad's personal life was unraveling, he continued to press forward and put on a brave face. For every huge—"uge" as he pronounced it—misstep he made with our family, he tried to counteract it with an act of bravery, a random kindness, a heroic action for someone else or undertaking some extraordinary feat of physical and mental toughness.

He jumped off an overpass bridge in Oxnard to save a girl and her younger brother who were on the verge of drowning.

He ran 56 miles in one day for this 56th birthday. When I called him "Iron Man" he corrected me—"Psycho Boy!"

When Waikiki was being evacuated after being placed on a tsunami warning, Dad texted me a picture of himself standing alone on the empty beach of Waikiki—*The best time to hit the beach and avoid tourists is during a tsunami!*

He bought a hundred hamburgers at McDonalds and personally delivered them to homeless people on Skid Row in downtown Los Angeles just because.

While working as a private investigator, he helped to identify and capture the stalker of a world-famous celebrity.

He helped a girlfriend evict alleged mobsters and money launderers from her rental property.

He took multiple groups of people hiking to the top of Mount Whitney and acted as their trail guide.

He walked multiple nieces down the aisle on their wedding days.

He joined the Coast Guard Auxiliary.

He once took us to the workshop of a suspected murderer, as part of a covert operation to get the murderer to confess.

He flew to China to help build a bat-making machine at the Louisville Slugger factory, just to help a friend.

He wrote and self-published his own "fact-based fiction" book to tell the stories of all his experiences as a parole officer.

He attempted to run for Governor of California under his own newly formed party, "The Common Centrist Party." Membership, one. He missed getting his name on the ballot because of a small technicality—something he insisted was the result of a vengeful person from his past.

When his sister was diagnosed with cancer, he spent countless hours finding her housing, going to her doctor's appointments, tracking down organic herbal remedies and getting her the best care possible at a world-class cancer treatment facility.

But most of the time, while he was out doing these heroic things, the rest of us were left wondering where he was and what he was doing. We always learned about these solo adventures after the fact. He never thought about how his behavior might impact the rest of us. The most glaring example of this occurred during the Montecito Mudslides in 2018.

In December 2017, the Thomas Fire started near our small town in Southern California, and the hot Santa Ana winds caused the fire to rapidly expand across the state, quickly becoming the largest fire in California history at the time. The fire burned for a month—destroying thousands of homes and decimating hundreds of thousands of acres of brush in the process. Fire crews finally contained the fire on January 12, 2018.

In early January 2018, before the fire was fully contained, a rainstorm hit Ventura and Santa Barbara counties; residents were warned about potential flashfloods and mudslides. At the time, Dad was living in Montecito in his latest girlfriend's house. Montecito is an incredibly wealthy part of Santa Barbara County, home to celebrities from Oprah to Ellen DeGeneres, tech billionaires, royalty, and more.

Although California had been in a drought for several years, the timing of this rainstorm was less than ideal. As a result of the Thomas Fire, the Santa Ynez Mountains that bordered the two counties had been stripped bare of their vegetation. Without the local vegetation, the soil covering the steep mountainside became loose and unstable.

Over the course of two days, more than four inches of rain fell. Because the ground was charred and stripped of vegetation, the water had nowhere to go but downhill—toward all the houses below.

On January 9, 2018, I woke up to the horrific news that the rainstorm had caused catastrophic mudslides in Montecito. Early that morning, the Santa Ynez creek had filled with an unprecedented amount of water, overflowed, and turned into an unruly and deadly river. Boulders the size of cars traveled down the canyon, crushing houses and their human occupants. A river of mud and debris flowed through the idyllic neighborhoods, ripping through houses and sweeping over sprawling estates. Dozens of houses were instantly demolished by the wind, water, and mud. Parents were ripped away from their children, as the mud sucked them under and carried their lifeless bodies away.

The creek that turned into a river was directly across the street from the house where Dad had been living with his then-girlfriend. I was glued to the TV, watching images of houses on their street covered in mud up to the roof, and I could not get in touch with

Dad. The body count on the news kept increasing—two dead, three dead, eight dead. Still no word from Dad.

Panic bubbled in my chest as I tried calling Dad's phone. It rang and rang with no answer. His voice mailbox had been full for as long as I could remember, so I couldn't even leave him a message.

In my panic, I tried calling in a favor with my old co-workers at the Santa Barbara Police Department. Had any of them seen or heard from Dad? Could they please let me know if they found his body before I somehow saw it on the news?

For days, I waited to hear from Dad, from his girlfriend, from a former colleague, from the police—from anyone about his whereabouts.

Finally, my phone lit up with his name. He was finally calling me.

Dad didn't apologize for not contacting me sooner. He didn't understand why I was so worried about him. In fact, he was calling to see if I had seen his mention in the Washington Post?

When I finally found the article, I understood why he wanted me to read it: once again, he had looked danger straight in the face and refused to back down.

"Near the base of Cold Spring Creek, Boris Romanowsky, 59, shook his head as he surveyed the damage. Romanowsky, a former firefighter, said he refused to evacuate and was checking on neighbors who, like him, had no power or water.

> 'The noise was so loud you could hardly hear yourself think. We had fire on the eastern sky before sunrise and we had this train wreck of a river going through at the same time. We had rain so loud you could hardly see.
>
> Despite the forecasts for more rain in the coming weeks, he has no plans to leave.
>
> 'I monitor the transistor radio,' he said. "I've been here since the first fire. I don't evacuate."

I was proud of his bravery, and also frustrated that he couldn't understand how afraid I had been during those days. At the same time, I was upset with *myself* for worrying so much. I knew Dad made it out of every crazy situation he was ever in, just like a modern-day superhero. So why did my body always betray me? Why did my anxiety always cause me to doubt that he'd make it?

In the end, twenty-three people died in the Montecito mudslide. Thankfully, Dad was not one of them.

PART III

17

THE CALL - OCTOBER 28, 2020

M ost parents of young children would agree that the hours between dinnertime and bedtime move at a glacial pace. Every night, it is the same routine. Dinner. Clean-up. Bath. Bed. Repeat. Even a global pandemic couldn't change that fact pattern.

So, when Dad called me at 6:30 that evening, I ignored it. He knew better than to call in the thick of the evening madness. I pressed "IGNORE" and sent him to voicemail. I'd call him back later.

He called again immediately. Natalie wailed at the dinner Rob was trying to feed her. Again, I pressed IGNORE and sent him to voicemail. This time getting frustrated. *He's probably drinking*, I thought.

My phone buzzed with a text message:

Boomer, please call me. From Dad.

Shit, maybe it *was* serious.
I texted back:

I am getting the kids ready for bed—can I call you in an hour?

Yes, but don't forget.

Alarm swept in. Funny how a moment of annoyance can so quickly change into a moment of panic, with just a few short words.

As Rob cleaned up the dinner table, I rushed through the bedtime routine with the kids, snapping at them to hurry up. Suddenly, there was nothing more important than getting them to sleep so I could call Dad back.

Eventually, the kids fell asleep, and I escaped back downstairs. I made a half-assed attempt to put the toys away before I collapsed onto the floor and called Dad. My back was slumped against the wall. I set my phone on speaker so Rob could listen also.

Dad answered right away. I don't know what I was expecting, but it wasn't this:

"I have cancer again."

With everything that our family had been through in 2005, I shouldn't have been shocked, but I was. Dad was extremely vigilant about his annual cancer screenings. As far as I knew, every single one was normal, until now. He was strong, he was healthy, he was invincible. Or so I thought.

Dad kept talking: "I could tell right away that something was up... the doctor was poking around for longer than usual during my last colonoscopy. You know, I don't think it's that bad. Probably just a small tumor or something that they can remove. They're going to send me for a PET scan tomorrow to check it out and I will keep you posted. Don't say anything to your sister until we learn more..."

"I'm sure it's going to be okay," Dad said.

But it wasn't okay. A few days later, on November 5, 2020, Dad called again.

It wasn't just a small tumor. The cancer was all over. The stomach. The liver. The rectum. The lungs. Stage IV. Inoperable. The words spun around in my brain.

"Yeah, I guess it's pretty bad when the surgical oncologist is crying when she tells you its incurable and inoperable..." Dad made a weak attempt at a joke before the line fell silent, and I knew in that moment that he was crying.

"I am so sorry, Dad..." I squeaked out. I pushed my own pain and confusion aside and rushed to comfort him.

But Dad didn't know how to accept emotional support. It was never part of our relationship. He was tough. He was strong. He was invincible. At least, that's how he wanted to present himself. But deep down (or not that deep down) I think he was a scared boy needing comfort. Needing someone to tell him it was going to be all right.

I later learned that between those two phone calls, he had called Mom. They had been divorced for a decade, yet in this frightening time, when he came face-to-face with his own mortality, he turned to her for guidance.

"It's really bad, Kelly. I don't think I can tell our children. I don't think they should know. I can't tell them."

"They aren't children anymore, Boris. You owe it to them to tell them the truth. They can handle it and they can help you. You don't have to do this alone."

THE DAYS after the initial diagnosis were some of the loneliest of my life. My sister and I are incredibly close, and we share a great bond. But we both handled Dad very differently. At the time of Dad's diagnosis, she and Dad hadn't spoken in a few months, after he totally lost his cool with her one night and sent her a slew of belligerent emails. I was still going to my support group and trying to learn how to maintain healthy boundaries with an active alcoholic.

When he called to tell me the prognosis, he also gave me my marching orders: "Yeah, it would be good if you called your sister and told her for me," he instructed. "I don't know why we haven't spoken in a few months; I am not mad at her!"

He was totally and completely oblivious to the fact that perhaps *she* was mad at *him*. Or maybe he wasn't oblivious; maybe he was just in denial. Whatever the case—it then became *my* job to tell my sister that our dad had received a terminal diagnosis.

And so, just as I had always done in the past, I rose to the occasion. I called Launa and delivered the news. On that day, the two of us began to walk this journey of our father's terminal cancer diagnosis. And though we were in it together, truthfully, I always felt alone. I felt alone in my sadness and despair. I felt that I couldn't be honest about how sad I was, because I knew that her feelings about Dad and his diagnosis were more complex than mine.

I fell into an age-old pattern: discarding my own feelings to protect the feelings of those around me. I wanted to be respectful of the fact that her relationship with Dad wasn't the same as mine, and maybe she didn't always want to hear about how heartbroken I was. So, I kept a lot of it inside. Sure, I shared with her my worries. But my sadness? My fears? My anguish? That I mostly kept to myself.

It almost ate me alive.

THE WEEKS after Dad's diagnosis were full of uncertainty. One minute, he was discussing driving to City of Hope to get top-of-the-line treatment. The next minute, he was considering not doing any treatment at all. I remember hearing the phrase "three months" and doing the math, counting back to the day we first learned he was sick. If he wasn't going to do any treatment at all, I needed to start mentally preparing for him to die. On the other hand, if he was going to start treatment, I needed to prepare for the side effects: hair loss, fatigue, nausea. But I also needed to prepare for the victories— maybe he *could* beat it!

Back and forth. Up and down. Round and round, he went. Each day, something different.

Eventually, he decided to fight it with everything he had and in January 2021, he went to Cottage Hospital to have a chemotherapy port inserted into his chest.

My emotions were hitched to his decisions. I held on for dear life and in the process, over the next two and a half years, I got dragged.

18

THE INSURANCE POLICY

In 2008, Breaking Bad aired for the first time. Walter White, a mediocre high-school science teacher, is slapped upside the head with a devastating cancer diagnosis in his mid-forties. When he is forced to face his mortality head-on, he begins to panic about what his family will do without him and stresses about his ability to provide for them after his death. Struggling to generate cash quickly, Walt begins to manufacture methamphetamine.

Though his meth cooking starts innocuously enough, over the seasons we see Walt's character change as his motivations change. What started out as a lucrative, albeit unconventional, way of creating quick, extra cash for his family, slowly turns more sinister as Walt's motivations shift away from his family and toward himself. As he continues to defy the odds of his cancer diagnosis, it becomes clear that Walt is acting in his own self-interests, rather than the interests of his family.

Dad never started manufacturing methamphetamine to care for us after his death, but he *did* make some erratic decisions that he claimed were "for the family"—but ultimately, I knew were for him. One of those was the decision to cash in his life insurance policy.

DAD HAD DECIDED to start chemotherapy and fight his cancer diagnosis head on. In hindsight, it's puzzling why any of us ever doubted that he would do so—when had he ever given up anything without a fight?

In mid-April, after a few rounds of chemotherapy, he told me he needed to talk about his insurance policy.

Dad had been lucky enough to secure an excellent $500,000 life insurance policy when he was in his mid-forties, before he was diagnosed with cancer for the first time. The policy was a twenty-year term, and though the term wouldn't expire at the end of the twenty years, the premium would jump from an insignificant amount to an amount that was too expensive for him to afford.

In the years since my parents' divorce, Dad had jumped around from place to place, living with whatever girlfriend he was dating at the time. He frequently commented on the expensive housing market and how he couldn't afford anything in our area anymore. But he never, ever asked for anything from us—especially not money.

This time, things were different.

One night, he came over for dinner—another El Pollo Loco night. Per usual, Dad ate most of the chicken breasts and all the Pico de Gallo. When he finished his plate, he turned to the girls' plates and began to pick the broccoli and extra chicken pieces off theirs also. "Ya weren't gonna eat that, were ya?" was the famous line he would always say as he reached his fork across our plates and stabbed at the remnants of our meals. Side effect of growing up poor —you took food whenever you could get it.

Once he was finished eating, he gathered everyone's plates and napkins and cleared the table—meticulously picking up every grain of Mexican rice and every tortilla crumble.

I sent the girls outside to play and sat back down to talk

business. Dad was gearing up for the fight of his life against this cancer and according to him, he needed to get his "financial house in order." He then shared with us two big revelations: the premium on his life insurance was going up to $700/month, and he had about $20,000 in credit card debt.

Dad had always been diligent in teaching me about finances. He taught me about credit cards, loans, and interest rates at a young age. He taught me about putting money in retirement accounts as early as possible so I could get the benefits of long-term compounding interest. He always instructed me to "pay myself first" by putting money in savings immediately before spending anything. But somewhere along the line, I learned that Dad's advice was very much "do as I say, not as I do."

In the years since he retired from his job as a parole officer, he continued to work odd jobs as a private investigator to help supplement his income. But with the chemotherapy treatments piling up every ten days, he knew that he wouldn't be able to work anymore of his "side gigs" for much longer, so he needed a little extra help sorting out his finances.

It was then that he told us about Coventry. Somehow, this small company learned that Dad had a terminal diagnosis and reached out to him about selling his life insurance policy. They knew the premium was high and his life expectancy was low, and they were willing to take that gamble for the big payoff of $500,000. They offered him pennies on the dollar to buy the insurance policy from him during his lifetime. They would pay Dad $130,000 cash, and Dad would sign over the policy to them so that when he died, Coventry would receive the $500,000. A return on investment for them of hundreds of thousands of dollars. Dad, feeling desperate for money, was considering it.

He brought the paperwork over to the kitchen table, and we discussed finances. He was embarrassed at his amount of debt and worried he wouldn't be able to continue to live off his pension (well, *half* a pension, as he once again reminded us. As if the divorce had happened just yesterday and not twelve years prior.) Half a pension was doable when he was still capable of working odd jobs, but not when he was doing chemotherapy every ten days.

And so, he was considering selling this life insurance policy for cash. Dad rarely asked me for my advice, but for whatever reason he wanted to know my opinion.

My opinion was that this plan made no sense. Why on earth would you cash out a life insurance policy after a *terminal* diagnosis? Who cares about paying back credit card debt when your life is going to end soon anyway? So what if you refuse to pay them and get bad credit? You can't take a credit score into the afterlife. But at the same time, I didn't feel that I could come out and say all of that so bluntly. After all, I didn't want Dad to feel like I was giving up on him this early into his diagnosis.

Though I thought his plan made no sense, I was honored that Dad at least came to me first. Rather than belittle him by telling him how dumb I thought his idea was, Rob and I offered to help him instead.

It was clear that Dad hadn't wanted to ask us for help, but that he was relieved when we offered. "Oh!" he said with feigned surprise. "Well, um, if you are able to help ol' Dadio out, that would be cool-io. You know, I have never asked anybody for money in my whole life..."

That night, Rob and I came up with a plan: we would pay the monthly insurance premiums for him and loan him $30,000 to stay afloat while he was undergoing treatment. When he died, and his life insurance policy went into effect, we could recoup the $30,000 and the out-of-pocket expenses for the premium, and split the rest of the policy with my sister.

Loaning Dad $30,000 would almost wipe out our entire cash savings. It was the most money Rob and I had ever saved, and we hadn't exactly anticipated loaning it to Dad. But we felt honored to be able to do so, to give Dad some dignity in what we thought might be his final months.

Dad left that night seeming a little lighter—the relief evident in his eyes.

A FEW WEEKS LATER, Dad called to ask me to drive him to his doctor's appointment in Santa Barbara. I had never once taken him to a doctor's appointment. He always drove himself. Once, he even rode his bike 35 *miles* to the chemotherapy infusion appointment, just to prove he was "still tough." Mission accomplished.

So, I knew he must be feeling *extraordinarily* bad if he called me to ask for help again. I immediately rushed over to the studio where he was staying in Ventura. When I got to his place, he was sitting in a recliner, covered in a heated blanket. I was shocked that he wasn't well enough to even come to the door when I knocked. The door was a mere five steps from the chair. He looked pale and fatigued. It was the first time I had seen him display any kind of effect from the cancer, and I honestly thought he might die that day.

I grabbed his hand—something I *never* did—and told him I was going to take care of him. He squeezed my hand back, with tears pooling in the corners of his blue eyes. He discreetly lifted his hand to wipe a tear, muttering something under his breath about spring allergies. His large, strong hands looked ashy. He used the knuckle of his bent pointer finger to wipe the tear as he cleared his throat.

His hands had always intrigued me. Dad could never straighten his fingers all the way. If you looked close enough, you could see that his fingers were always slightly curved, as though his hands were locked in the ergonomically correct keyboard position.

I helped Dad to the car and drove him to his doctor in Santa Barbara. When they checked him at the oncologist's office, his oxygen levels were so low that they immediately asked me to take him to the Emergency Room to check his lungs.

We got back in my car, and I rushed him to the ER. This was still during the COVID protocols and so when we got to the ER, we had to pull up to the entrance and do the intake through the closed car window. When they finished the intake and Dad was supposed to get out of the car and go inside, he hunched over in the front seat and started fidgeting.

The nurse knocked on the window and yelled to see if he was going to get out. I started to panic that he was having a stroke or something because he was acting so strangely.

"Dad? You need to get out of the car and go inside."

All the sudden he looked over at me and said, "Don't tell anybody you have this!" and jumped out of the car quick as a cat.

I was totally confused, until I looked down to see that Dad had thrown a handgun onto the floorboard of my car.

Now—seeing as how I am, in Dad's words, a "woke-a-saurus"—I do not routinely carry handguns with me, and I was totally petrified of what on earth I was supposed to do with this new accessory. Who brings a handgun to a doctor's appointment? A retired parole officer, that's who. As with most experiences in life with Dad, I *shouldn't* have been shocked, and yet I was.

Because of the strict COVID-19 protocols in place at the time, I wasn't allowed to go into the hospital with Dad. Instead, I drove around the corner to sit in my car while I waited for a doctor to see him in the ER. I was so exhausted by the whole event that I fell asleep in my car. When I woke up, my car battery had died. Now I had a dad in the ER, a dead car battery *and* an unlicensed handgun in my center console. (To be clear, my dad had a license for the handgun, but I did not.)

I spent the rest of the afternoon trying to find someone to jump-start my car and panicking that I was going to be arrested for possession of a firearm. All the while, waiting to get news from the ER about what was wrong with Dad's lungs.

As it turns out, there was nothing inherently wrong with Dad (other than, of course, the fact that he had stage IV cancer). When he went in for his chemo infusion the day before, the oncologist had given him the same dose of chemo that he had for the prior two rounds, without considering that Dad had lost twelve pounds. In essence, they had accidentally overdosed him on chemotherapy. Nevertheless, I insisted the hospital keep him overnight for observation, just in case.

The next morning, after a night full of IV fluids, Dad was fine. In hindsight, the whole day was so bad, it was comical. But it didn't feel very funny then. I had started the morning devastated, thinking my dad was going to die that day. I spent the second half of the day incredibly angry with Dad for putting me in the uncomfortable situation of holding his stupid handgun. And went to bed that night annoyed that he was going to be fine after the IV fluids.

Yes, as guilty as I feel admitting it, I was *annoyed* that he was going to be "okay."

I was exasperated. Frustrated. Angry. I had wasted a whole day away from my work, from my husband, from my children, for what? Because a doctor had given him too much chemotherapy?

Of course, I was glad that Dad wasn't going to die that day. But I was emotionally exhausted. After decades of suppressing my emotions, they were coming at me from every which way, and I didn't know how to deal with them. I was trying to be present and in-the-moment, but that was taxing. As I waited for Dad in my car outside the hospital—thinking he might be on death's door—I felt tiny pieces of my heart shatter.

Over the next two years of Dad's illness, my heart continued to slowly splinter. Each CAT scan he received, each chemo treatment planned or rescheduled, each consult he had with another doctor—my emotions swirled and spiraled.

I was constantly in fight-or-flight mode, always waiting for the other shoe to drop.

19

SECOND-GUESSING

Because of how quickly the cancer had metastasized and spread throughout Dad's body, the doctors had to put him on an extremely intense and toxic form of chemotherapy. They told us that most patients could tolerate this type of chemotherapy for a maximum of six rounds. We were told from the beginning that this chemotherapy would never save Dad's life; it would only extend his life for as long as he could tolerate the treatment.

By July, Dad had surpassed his eighth round of chemotherapy. Not only had he surpassed the "maximum number of rounds," but he passed them with flying colors. Other than the accidental chemo overdose incident, Dad didn't get knocked out by the chemotherapy. He still went to the gym almost every day, sometimes—often—while wearing his chemotherapy pump.

He thought he was really beating the cancer. And in a sense, he was. There was no doubt that he was surpassing every doctor's expectation for both his quality of life and his life expectancy. He would tell us (*ad nauseum*) that he was the only cancer patient who got *more* hair while doing chemotherapy. And it was true—his eyelashes grew longer, and his full head of hair that had been stick-straight his entire life grew long and wavy.

He thought he knew more than the doctors. He thought they were wrong in telling him he was terminal. He was angry that they didn't give him options for holistic treatment. He was frustrated that they didn't ever want to talk about the importance of diet, exercise, and positive thinking. He was doing all those things—eating healthily and exercising—and because of this, he truly felt that the cancer was shrinking. And because of this, he got cocky.

A FEW WEEKS LATER, an email arrived in my inbox. In true Dad fashion, the subject line of the email was almost as long as the email itself:

> **To**: daughter@gmail.com
> **From**: Father@gmail.com
> **Re**: Coventry. Not for sharing. They sent me a written offer of 166,000 today. For your review and your records. We will talk later this week.
> **Message**: Please do not share this with anybody at this time. This is between you and me. Not even Launa at this time. Bargaining for my Life is a sensitive situation! Love Dad.

My mind reeled. What was he doing? Why was he still talking to Coventry? We had already resolved this issue—at least, I thought we had. I had given him $30,000 and was paying the monthly life insurance premiums. Why was Coventry still in the picture?

The answer came shortly thereafter, in another email.

> **To**: daughter@gmail.com
> **From**: Father@gmail.com
> **Re**: Coventry. Not for sharing. They sent me a written offer

of 166,000 today. For your review and your records. We will
talk later this week.
***Message**: My situation might become complex. It seems*
everybody except me thinks I'm not going to make it. I think
that I am going to beat this cancer contrary to popular
opinion. I expected my CAT Scan to be precisely what it is. I
knew that my lungs would be clear, and I expected my liver
to be clear or nearly clear. I was correct on both accounts. My
eyes are clear, my urine is clear, I have no abdominal pain.
My blood work is nearly perfect!

Dad, the narcissistic cancer patient. It is true that he was doing much better than the doctors had ever anticipated, but they had always said that chemo was to hold back the cancer, never to cure it. Yet here Dad was, months after he started chemo, declaring that he was going to "beat" cancer.

I felt trapped and confused. I didn't want to trample his dreams and stifle his motivation, but I also didn't want to live in a land of delusional grandeur. I believe in miracles, but I also believe in science.

I didn't know how to navigate this situation. There are no manuals for how to deal with an overly optimistic (narcissistic), terminally ill parent. Even now, it's hard to explain to people who didn't know him and who weren't there.

He thought he was going to beat cancer, and so, notwithstanding the fact that I had just given him $30,000 six weeks before, he was once again considering selling his $500,000 life insurance policy to Coventry.

I soon learned that he wasn't only "considering" it—he was actively negotiating with Coventry. In fact, he had never stopped negotiating with Coventry even *after* I gave him the $30,000. He was proud that he had negotiated a price of $166,000 instead of the $130,000 they had initially offered.

And yet, he wanted me to keep it secret. To not tell my sister, one of the closest people in my life. Dad always wanted to make things difficult. To do things in secret. It put me in a very uncomfortable position on multiple levels.

But Dad soon realized that he couldn't keep this secret from my sister for long. Since he had listed my sister and me as the beneficiaries on the life insurance policy, he couldn't sell it without us signing off.

The following weekend, my sister came to visit, and we went and saw Dad. We got to his studio, sat on the bed opposite his recliner chair and began sharing about our weeks.

After a few minutes, Dad leaned over in his chair and handed me a pink folded-up sticky note. He said nothing.

I opened it slowly. As I read his handwritten words, I could instantly feel the heat rising through my body. Splotches forming on my chest.

You are not coming to visit. You are coming to talk about the insurance. It was dated two days before our visit. He must have written it the day I called to tell him we wanted to come see him.

My sister looked over at me, confused at the sudden change in my demeanor.

"Well, it's true, right? I am not an idiot," Dad answered without my saying anything.

I was simultaneously embarrassed and enraged. The words in that small note ripped through me like fire. Shame and guilt spread through me as I quickly attempted to gather my thoughts.

"I already had the trip to Ventura planned, Dad," Launa quickly retorted after she read the note over my shoulder. "This wasn't a trip specifically to talk about the insurance. Of course, I think it is important to talk about it... But that's not why we're here."

Guilt flooded through me. Now, not only did Dad think we came just to talk about the insurance policy, but now he also knew that I had told my sister what he was doing, even when he explicitly told me not to. I felt like a child cowering in the corner. Being scolded. And shamed. So much shame.

Years later, I would reflect on this moment. Why did I feel so much shame and guilt? This shouldn't have even been my secret to keep in the first place. If Dad wanted to keep it private, he could have. It wasn't my job to keep his secrets. But of course, I didn't think that in the moment because I was too wrapped up in my own misplaced guilt to think or see straight.

We knew why Dad wanted to cash out the insurance policy—he wanted to buy a house. Ever since he and Mom got divorced, he had never stopped talking about how expensive real estate was. Now, thanks to Coventry, a down payment would fall into his lap. And here's the thing—we *wanted* Dad to have a house if that's what he wanted for himself. But not if that was simply what he wanted for us.

For years, Dad had talked about his dream of owning a house in the woods. A family cabin for building generational wealth. He was obsessed with having something physical, something tangible, to pass on to us. But that was his dream, not ours. We didn't want a second house in the woods to maintain. We weren't financially stable enough to have a "second house." We didn't *need* a second house to remember him by—and for years, even before he got sick, we had told him that. We tried to impress upon him that if he wanted to cash out his life insurance to buy a house to live out the rest of his life in comfort, or if he wanted to cash it out to experience bucket-list items or to travel, we were all for it and supported him one-hundred percent. But, if he was cashing out the policy to buy a house just so he could "leave us" a house as a legacy—we didn't want or need that.

The only places he wanted to buy were far away and would be difficult for us to manage, financially and logistically after he passed. We'd benefit so much more from the cash from the life insurance policy. We could use it to send all his grandchildren to college.

Something that was unimaginable for *his* parents. He could secure his generational legacy through his grandchildren.

But he wasn't listening. He grew increasingly angry. His blue eyes seared. "Well, if you won't sign off on the sale of the insurance, I will just change the beneficiary to Anita and tell her to sign off. I don't need your permission. I can change the beneficiary to anybody I want."

It was a slap in the face. We had just expressed ourselves vulnerably, and instead of listening to our perspectives, he grew hostile and inflexible. Not only that, but he threatened to remove us entirely in place of his old girlfriend from ten years ago. He knew those words would sting.

This was the Dad I had always feared. The angry one, the obstinate one. We better get in line or get out of his way.

A FEW DAYS LATER, an email from Dad at 2:32 a.m.

> **To**: daughter@gmail.com
> **From**: Father@gmail.com
> **Re**: Coventry Forms to Sign
> **Message**: I think we are going to end up ahead on this. I would be much happier living in my own place that will be part of your long-term real estate portfolio and generational wealth. Who knows…If I can buy In SLO County…This might be where your daughters live while going to college at Cal Poly! I am comfortable with selling now. I don't think that I am going to die as soon as everybody thinks.
> respectfully submitted, Dear old Dad.

We signed the forms consenting to the sale, and he sold the policy for $166,000 on July 10, 2021.

SHALLOW WATERS

To: daughter@gmail.com
From: Father@gmail.com
Re: *Gramps on top of the Chilnuahlna Falls, the 2nd tallest waterfall in Yosemite! Near Wawona Hotel. 5 miles up hill...both ways!*
Message: *This was a 5 mile hike uphill last Friday! I had 5 more downhill. Not bad for an aging over the hill terminal cancer patient!*

To: Father@gmail.com
From: daughter@gmail.com
Re: *Gramps on top of the Chilnuahlna Falls, the 2nd tallest waterfall in Yosemite! Near Wawona Hotel. 5 miles up hill...both ways!*
Message: *Wow, that's beautiful! Don't forget to write down all your favorite hiking spots so I can share them with the girls.*

People often dream of California summers—beautiful sandy beaches, sparkling blue water and sunny skies. But we natives know that the summer months are full of a persistent haze and June gloom. The beautiful weather comes in the fall. Beach days can stretch into September and even early October, until eventually we beg for the sun to go away for a bit so we can drink cozy drinks and curl up under blankets watching spooky movies.

It was an extraordinarily hot October day, and Rob, the girls and I went hiking with Dad to one of his favorite places in Montecito. He didn't want to write down his favorite spots, he wanted to show us. Dad didn't care that my kids were only four and two—he expected them to hike, too.

A quarter mile into the hike, the trail crossed a small creek. Though it had been a dry year, a steady stream of water flowed over small mossy rocks. My daughter tossed a rock into the stream, and as it collided with another smaller rock, I shuddered. It was hard to believe that the gentle stream we were looking at was the same one that had swelled to record heights and rushed through the surrounding neighborhoods, killing twenty-three people just three years earlier.

As we prepared to cross the creek and reconnect to the trail, Dad motioned us to follow him upstream along the creek bed instead. Out of the corner of my eye, I noticed Rob giving me a look of uncertainty. He had recently had foot surgery and was already nervous about hiking—he hadn't signed up for scaling rocks too.

My children climbed like lizards, gripping the boulders—their chubby fingers and toes not yet free of the soft baby fat. I followed close behind, trying to take it all in.

As I crested the last big boulder, I looked down to see a spot where the creek had formed a perfect circle of water. Rob came up behind me and sat down. He couldn't make it any further. Dad helped the girls down to the pond.

"This is for you girls—I made it! A natural swimmin' hole!" Dad boasted as he looked at my kids with pride.

While the rest of the world had largely stayed inside during the COVID-19 Pandemic of 2020, Dad had hiked up this creek daily. He found the smoothest and flattest rocks and layered them around the pool to make room for us to sit.

In that moment, time slowed as I realized I was watching my dad relive my childhood and his own young fatherhood. Exploring creeks, searching for critters and guiding us to secret swimming spots. I saw myself in my daughters—blindly trusting their grandpa to lead them on their next big adventure.

I didn't know how many more hikes we would have with Dad, and so I nudged Rob to grab his iPhone to video the moment of our girls with their grandpa. I didn't want to forget it, and I didn't want them to forget either.

But what he ended up capturing on that video wasn't what I had planned at all. It wasn't anything that I wanted to remember.

It happened so quickly.

A gasp, followed by a large splash. A flash of pink under the water. *She can't swim! Don't panic.*

Moments before my two year old fell into the pond.

Dad is right there. He's reaching down to grab her. He's reaching. He's reaching. Why isn't he grabbing? Why isn't he grabbing? She's right there. Grab her! The pink slowly sinking.

"Grab her head! Get her out of the water!" Rob shouted from behind me.

"Natalie!" I yelled.

"Don't worry, I got her—I got her."

A child's scream punctured the air, like a newborn emerging from the womb for the first time.

"Did you have a nice swim?" Dad said with a chuckle, lifting Natalie up from the pond and attempting to dissipate the fear, to downplay what had just happened.

But it was too late—I had seen. This wasn't the same Dad as my childhood. This Dad was dying inside, starting with the nerves in his hands.

21

DECOMPRESSING & DEMENTIA

Although Dad was one of ten siblings, by 2021, four were dead and he was only in contact with one of the other five. Because of the fractured nature of the family in his generation, he made a concerted effort to keep in contact with all his nieces and nephews. I think he felt a heightened sense of responsibility to watch out for the children of his siblings who had died—even though those children were all adults now, several of them with children of their own. He took great pride in all their successes and would brag about his nieces and nephews almost as much as his own children. He took on a self-appointed, quasi-parent role with many of them.

In October 2021, one of my cousins flew down from San Francisco to visit Dad. He planned for all of us to go to dinner in the harbor. No less than five minutes into dinner, Dad started telling us about a missing woman he was looking for and how he had tracked her down to a shanty near Skid Row. This news was shocking to me on many levels, not the least of which was that I thought he was no longer doing any private investigator gigs because of his chemotherapy treatments.

What we did not realize is that he had quite literally *just* tracked her down that day. The next thing we knew, a short and stout woman was standing at our table. Her hair was gray and frayed. She looked tired, but excited. She said, "Thank you so much for finding my daughter. Let's go get her, Boris!"

Dad scooted out his chair, threw a ten-dollar bill on the table and drove straight to Skid Row, leaving us to finish the dinner and pay for the rest of it by ourselves. To the woman, that day was miraculous—Boris found her missing daughter! To us, his behavior was inconsiderate—Dad unexpectedly left us in the middle of a family dinner, again.

ABOUT TWO WEEKS LATER, I received a phone call from a police officer, looking to speak to "the family of Boris Romanowsky." My mind raced and I felt sick. I thought he had been in a car accident or had gotten into an altercation with someone. Funnily enough, the idea that he might have died from cancer didn't immediately come to mind.

Internally, my blood pressure skyrocketed, and my chest tightened. But on the exterior, I looked and sounded composed. I had many years of experience in dealing with traumatic situations. It would take more than a phone call from a police officer to completely unravel my calm exterior.

"Yes, this is his daughter speaking. May I ask what this is regarding?" I responded.

Dad was not dead or injured. But he was with the police—not in their custody, but under their observation. After the officer confirmed my dad was not dead or injured, he started to ask me questions about his mental state and whether he had been diagnosed with dementia. I had heard a lot of crazy stories about my dad over the years, but this was the first time anybody had ever asked me if he had dementia.

When I inquired further, the officer said, "Well, your father is here in Los Osos, and he has been robbed—his car, his wallet and his gun were stolen."

The officer continued, "But the story about why he is here and how this happened makes no sense, and we are very concerned about his mental health. When we asked your dad what he was doing in Los Osos, he told us that he had just rescued a missing woman from a shanty in Skid Row and that he came up here to decompress after he got paid for the gig. He thinks that the 'criminals who stole the girl' tracked him down and stole his car in revenge."

The officer then asked, "So, when was the last time your dad has seen a medical professional?"

I assured the officer that with Dad, often the truth was much stranger than fiction. Though he may have some wild stories, he did not have dementia. I confirmed for the police that he really did save a woman from Skid Row and that this was just another day in the life with my dad.

When I hung up the phone, a sense of relief flooded through me. Dad was okay.

Dad called me himself about an hour later to explain the situation. As the police had relayed to me, he had gone to Los Osos to decompress after he found the missing girl and returned her to her mother. But what he did after that was anybody's guess. He told me he just explored the town for a bit and then fell asleep in the hotel room. Because the hotel was so close to the beach, he decided to sleep with the door wide open so he could get a cool ocean breeze. When he woke up, he had been robbed. His wallet, his keys, his car and his gun had been stolen.

I believed him that he went to Skid Row to save the woman. I believed him that he went to Los Osos to decompress. I believe that he wandered around town by himself just to check it out. But I didn't believe it for a second that he voluntarily fell asleep with the door wide open for an ocean breeze. Dad *did* love the ocean breeze, but he was also no dummy. There's no way he would have left all his valuables in a hotel room and fallen asleep with the door wide open.

So what really happened? I suspect he got drunk and passed out. That he was still drinking while he was on hardcore chemotherapy boggled my mind. But I tried to remember, alcoholism is a disease. An alcoholic can't just cease drinking like a non-alcoholic can—even if they are dying of cancer.

THE POLICE FOUND Dad's car in Riverside a few days later. It had been stripped clean and spray-painted with graffiti. Maybe he was right about someone seeking revenge—the girl he "rescued" was from Riverside. Maybe she didn't want to be rescued after all.

A FEW MONTHS LATER, Dad's car was fixed and repainted. In early December, he came over for another night of El Pollo Loco. We spent several hours that evening eating and chatting. As he was walking through the garage to leave, he stopped and suddenly turned around and walked back toward me, as if he had forgotten something inside.

But he hadn't forgotten anything. Except to tell me something of monumental importance.

"Oh, I forgot to tell you. I bought a house in Washington. I'm moving there after the New Year."

I stared at him in shock. My mind reeled—*Washington State? As in, two states away from where we currently live?*

But all I could manage to squeak out was, "Wow, that's a big deal."

"It will be our new family compound! Where all the grandkids and cousins can go to visit," he continued.

What about his treatment? What about us? How is he going to get there? I thought.

He answered as if he could read my mind.

"I am going to move up there after the first of the year with my old buddy from high school, Marty. I'm going to take a break from treatment for a while. The house is a fixer-upper, so I am going to spend the next six months getting the house ready and then I want the whole family—all the cousins too—to come visit for the Fourth of July!"

None of this made any sense to me. His treatment had been going well—why would he stop it? The doctors had said that he was terminal—why would he move two states away from his entire family at the end of his life?

I had stopped going to therapy years before, but after Dad's re-diagnosis in October, I had immediately called my old therapist. Thankfully, she was able to fit me back into her schedule, and I had been going regularly the past few months.

A couple days later, I was talking with her on the phone, telling her about Dad's plan to move to Washington. "Why would he do this? None of this makes any sense!" I lamented.

"As goes the wedding, so goes the divorce," she responded.

My face scrunched and my eyebrows raised. "Huh?"

"It's a saying that basically means, how one person acts now is an indicator of how they will act in the future. Of course your dad's behavior doesn't make sense. Your dad has *never* done things in a way that makes sense to you. Just because he is dying, doesn't mean that he's a different person who is going to start acting differently."

That was a hard truth for me to accept. I was angry that he was moving to Washington. I didn't understand how he could do that to his kids and his grandkids. Didn't he need us to help him through this last phase of his life? Didn't he want to be around us as much as possible before he died? Who was going to take care of him when he got sick? How would we know if he was declining? It was often too much for me to bear emotionally. Because at the end of the day, beneath all my anger and confusion, was immense sadness. The pain of knowing that my dad didn't *want* to be around us as much as possible.

On top of this, I didn't know how to explain it to others. When people found out he was moving to Washington, the first thing they would always ask was, "Do you have family up there?' or "Is that where he is from?" No and no. Aside from going to a softball tournament in Central Washington in the late 1990s, we had never even vacationed in Washington.

But as promised, Dad moved to Washington in January 2022. Not just any place in Washington—the northernmost part of Washington—as far north as you can go before hitting Canada. He stopped all chemotherapy treatments and focused all his efforts on taking care of the new house. He would send text messages of the progress almost daily. Picture of himself mowing the lawn. Picture of himself building compost boxes in the yard. Picture of himself standing in the sand during low tide at Birch Bay. Picture of himself measuring and hanging drywall. He never stopped moving.

In hindsight, I can now see that he was doing what he had always taught us to do—keep moving. He had to keep moving so he wouldn't crash. He had to keep moving because that's all he knew how to do. If he stopped moving, I think the weight of the situation would have killed him right then and there. He couldn't have handled the grief of actually *feeling* the realization that his own life was coming to an end.

But what he didn't see was that *I* couldn't push things away as well as he could. I couldn't keep running. I was in emotional-growth limbo. In the years after law school but before Dad got sick, I practiced un-learning the practice of my childhood of stuffing my emotions. I tried to practice *feeling* things. I tried practicing how to slow down and rest. But I was a work-in-progress and my learning was nowhere near done.

When Dad got sick, all the progress that I had made came to a screeching halt. I was caught in a whirlwind of emotions, and I only had half a toolbox full of tools to handle them. The unknowns constantly ran through my mind.

Where would I be when Dad died?

What would it look like?

Would I get to say goodbye?

Would he die in Washington alone?

Would he come back home?

I wasn't ready to fully stuff all my emotions, but I wasn't fully ready to feel them all, either. And the result was two years of anger and irritability. But beneath that was fear and anticipatory grief.

22

MY UNEXPECTED GUEST

"Take it easy on yourself."

"Adjust your expectations."

"Don't hide your grief."

These are the bits of advice that the internet spat out at me in response to my constant googling of: "How to parent while dealing with a dying parent."

In other words, completely useless.

After a year of dealing with Dad's failing health and erratic behavior, my expectations of myself as a mother were already at rock-bottom. More than once, my four-year-old had been sent home from preschool with borrowed underwear after she accidentally showed up to class in a skirt and a bare butt. We'd sent them to school with Starbucks snack packs as their food. Breakfast? Optional. Brushed hair? Don't care.

Someone asked me one day what size shoe my six-year-old wore. I had no idea. My mom had done all their back-to-school shopping that year.

Fatigue. Sadness. Brain fog. These are all things that can be "handled" by lowering expectations, outsourcing, and taking it easy.

But the articles don't tell you how to manage the rage.

I had never been an angry person, I had never been one to yell or scream—until then. The fiery anger inside of me was never far away. It lurked beneath the shadows, waiting to pounce. One sibling squabble, one four-year-old's refusal to brush her teeth, and it would rush out.

"BRUSH YOUR TEETH," I growled through clenched teeth.

My rage—an unwelcome guest that had taken residency in my home.

I didn't have this problem at work or in public. Sure, I would get irritated with people, but this rage? This rage was reserved for my children. It was my biggest source of shame. They didn't deserve it. I didn't want to do it—and yet, I struggled to control it.

My unrelenting headaches were a reminder of how hard I constantly clenched my jaw, exercising the extreme restraint it took for me to not throw or kick something. Sometimes, I did throw things. I am not proud.

Motherhood was brutally hard for me on a good day. Throwing in anticipatory grief and a dying parent made motherhood unbearable.

There was a short period of time before Dad got sick when all was well. I was never a Pinterest mom, or even an Instagram mom. But I was a mom. It was hard being a working mom, with a full-time job and two very young kids, but I was doing it.

When the pandemic hit in March 2020, our girls were two-and-a-half and nine months old. Of course, there were stressors during that time—the entire world was in disarray. But internally, I was doing well. I was able to manage the girls and do fun things with them, despite the chaos of the outside world.

But when Dad got sick in October 2020, everything changed. I was constantly on edge. Emotionally depleted. Exhausted. How could I parent small children and nurture their big feelings and emotions when I could barely understand my own? How could I be a loving parent and a distressed child at the same time?

I could put on a brave face to cope with the outside world, but I was unable to cope with my family. I lashed out at them. After hours of holding it together at work, I had nothing left to give when I came home.

But, instead of pulling back from work and my career to preserve more energy for my family, I did the opposite. I leaned into my career—hard.

After Dad's diagnosis in October 2020, I became an equity partner in my law firm. With my new law partners I bought, designed, and remodeled a new commercial office building. I helped choose the layout of the building, the design of the offices and the furniture. I was awarded and featured as a "40 under 40" recipient in the local newspaper. I presented an educational seminar to the local bar association in front of one-hundred of my peers and our local judge. I joined multiple networking groups. I became the co-Chair of the Estate Planning and Probate Section of the local bar association. I gave multiple seminars. I took on complex cases and was successful.

Why? Why did I lean into all of that rather than pull back? Because excelling in my career was easy for me. I know the law. I know how to handle a courtroom. I know how to handle clients and manage their expectations. I know how to be efficient and bill my time wisely. I know how to vet cases and how to handle opposing counsel. I know what works. I know how to problem-solve. I know how to measure my success in the office.

But you know what doesn't come naturally to me? Being a mother. I don't find great joy out of cooking a new meal for my kids or thinking of crafty things to do on a Saturday morning. Courtrooms have rules and procedures and stability—children do not. Children are unpredictable, volatile, messy, and exhausting. Their needs are unrelenting and their attitudes unpredictable.

The only way I knew how to deal with the chaos of my dad's

diagnosis and his behaviors was to lean into what I know how to do best—be a lawyer.

It was a vicious cycle. I focused more on my work to ignore the chaos of my dad's situation. But the more I focused on work, the less emotional energy I had for my family and children. The less energy I had for my children, the more they tried to suck it out of me. The more they tried to suck it out of me, the more I pulled back, exasperated by their parasitic nature. And thus, the cycle continued.

In motherhood, I constantly felt like I was failing—why would I lean into that?

23

WHIPLASH

January 16, 2022, a phone call from Dad. Voice gruff and rambling, slurring a bit.

"Sasha, do you know the date today? I need you to know the date today. It's January 16, 2022. I need you to remember this day. It is a very important day. My brother Roman died today. They found him frozen in the back of a van. I don't know if it was COVID or drugs or alcohol or what. But he's dead. My older brother, he's gone. Please, Sasha, just remember the date my brother Roman died —January 16, 2022."

Dad had been estranged from Roman for years, but his death still haunted him. As of January 2022, Dad had outlived five of his seven brothers.

As PROMISED, Dad stopped chemotherapy when he moved to Washington in January 2022. He spent his days fixing the house and exercising. He felt good. He thought he had outsmarted the doctors. He wasn't really dying. What dying man can go to the gym and lift weights every day? What dying man can hang drywall? No, he wasn't really dying. He had beat it.

Sometimes, even I believed it. How could I not? I really didn't know any other person with terminal cancer who could do all the things that Dad did. Maybe he was right. Maybe the doctors *were* wrong. Maybe the clean Washington air and the open space was healing him.

But four months later, in May 2022, Dad did a routine CAT scan, and I received another late-night email. Once again, the subject line told me all I needed to know:

> **To**: daughter@gmail.com
> **From**: Father@gmail.com
> **Re**: This is today's cat scan. The impressions at the bottom are also the conclusions. Widespread cancer throughout the peritoneal cavity. Staying in the fight! Love Dad
> **Message**: No text

He didn't even give me time to decide whether I wanted to open the email and read the news yet; he put it all in the subject line. Of *course*, the cancer was now widespread—he had stopped all treatment. It gutted me.

Dad's friend—who I secretly referred to as the "Mole"—called and told me that after the CAT scan results, the doctor told Dad he would be lucky to make it through the end of the year. I was sad and angry and confused. But we couldn't talk about these things on the phone, because Dad always avoided difficult conversations. So, I'd have to make do with email.

> **To**: Father@gmail.com
> **From**: daughter@gmail.com
> **Message**: I know you like to be strong and not scare us, but not having all the information about your condition is really

STOPPING TO FEEL | 177

*hard for me, and I just end up panicking. I know I usually
keep a very calm and straight face, but your health issues
have been really hard for me emotionally. I get upset and cry
a lot in the evenings and I get anxious and have panic attacks
during the days. I fully support whatever decisions you make
(treatment, no treatment, chemo, holistic, whatever), but I
don't like hearing things second-hand or piecemeal because it
feels like I never really know what's actually going on. It
would really help me cope if you could just give it to me
straight, so I'm not left guessing. So, I guess I'm asking: what
did the doctor say this time around? And what did he say to
expect with this chemo?*

__To__: daughter@gmail.com
__From__: Father@gmail.com
*__Message__: I feel fine right now and I am super strong and
training and working hard every day. I fully understand the
situation and diagnosis and I am not in any form of denial.
However, I still think I have a chance of pulling off or
participating in some sort of miracle. I think my diagnosis
says something like 97 percent likely to die. I plan on being
in the 3 percent that make it. Please do not stress or worry
about me. Under the circumstances I am doing well. If things
go South and I start going downhill I will modify my plans.
As of now I am good to go and looking forward to the 4th of
July in Blaine. It is a little beautiful portside town. I am sure
that you will all enjoy the visit and have fun. Love Dad.*

So that was it. I was just supposed to "not worry" about him.
The thing that upset me the most is that I don't think Dad had any
idea how his behavior affected the rest of us. If he was "doing well"
then he didn't understand why the rest of us weren't. We just had to
"not worry" about him and it would all be okay.

But it wasn't okay, and I did worry. I continued to agonize about his condition and whether he was telling us the whole truth. He never told us the whole truth his entire life, so why would he start now? But somehow, I thought this was different. We were adults now. We were dealing with his health.

After he died, I found his trusty *Day Timer* calendar where he tracked everything. Inside of it were notes about his condition. In these months when he told me he was fine, there were notes about throwing up blood. He never told us he was throwing up blood. He hid the whole truth from us—to protect us.

———

FROM MAY TO JULY 2022, Dad spent almost every waking minute doing things to fix up his house in Washington for our big Fourth of July trip. He was so excited for everyone to come. He was obsessed about it. He was constantly checking in on us to make sure we knew which airline to fly (Southwest or Allegiant!) which places to stay (Birch Bay or Semiahmoo!). The Mole texted me frequently:

> Your Dad is so excited for this cousins' day trip. Fixing up this house is giving him something to live for!

I was glad it was giving him something to live for, but why weren't *we* enough to live for? Why wasn't staying in California and being around his family enough to live for?

I honestly didn't know how I'd feel when I saw the house. Nobody but me and my sister knew how he had managed to purchase it. We never told anybody about the life insurance policy. It wasn't our story to tell. Although I was upset and angry inside about how it had all gone down, I was happy for him that he got his dream. I could never have lived with myself if I had prevented him from getting it—no matter how hurt I was that he was moving so far away.

I'd be lying, though, if I didn't admit that the whole situation brought up very thought-provoking questions. What *is* the role of a parent? Did he owe it to us to stay close by for our own comfort? If moving to Washington was what he truly wanted—should he do it, no matter the cost? I grappled with that question a lot.

I never felt like my dad "owed" me anything from a monetary standpoint. But he was my dad, and despite everything I knew about him and his behaviors, I still expected him to show up for me and provide me with emotional support. I expected him to be the "grown up" and make the right decisions. Deep down, despite everything I knew about him and his personality, I still had this sense that he should "know better" about certain things, a sense that he should act a certain way, say a certain thing, do a certain thing. I still thought, *He is the parent! How can he not see how this is hurting his children? How can he not be using this extra time he has been given to spend it with his family? His grandchildren? Why is he not comforting us?*

I learned later that expecting my dad to take care of my emotional needs was like going to the hardware store for bread—I was looking for something in the wrong store. I was never going to find it there. Dad couldn't fill those emotional needs for me because he simply did not know how.

There were many times that I resented him and that house. He got to escape to Washington to live out his fantasy and ignore the emotional pain of it all, while we were left to deal with the fallout. Dad had always stayed busy, charged forward, never stopping to feel the pain of whatever it was he was going through. In hindsight, this move to Washington was symbolic of the level of pain he was trying to stuff. He couldn't exercise this pain out. He literally had to physically move himself thousands of miles away from his family to try to get away from the pain.

While I was once angry at him for leaving us to move to Washington, there is now compassion. Maybe he couldn't spend a lot of time with us because it was too painful. He had to keep it short and keep moving. He wasn't purposely trying to hurt me or anybody else. He was doing the best he could with the tools he had, and the only tools he had for dealing with emotional pain were to keep moving—literally.

WE WENT to Washington for the Fourth of July, as Dad had requested. Seven cousins and their extended families joined us. There was no denying that the place was beautiful. Even in the middle of July, it was lush and green as far as the eye could see. The quaint town bubbled with friendly energy as little shops got ready for the Fourth of July parade. Wagons with streamers lined the streets, high schoolers set up face-painting tents and children ran wild and free on the streets. The smell of hot dogs and grilled corn filled the air and American Flags and colorful baskets of flowers hung from every street post. The sun stayed out late, creating an air of lightness late into the evening.

Dad's new house was very modest: an old mobile home converted to a single-family residence. Half of the rooms were unfinished, sheets hanging from the windows as curtains, and small mattresses tucked into corners. The living room had Dad's touches everywhere. Two large, unmatched couches filled the oversized room. Huge pieces of obscure art hung on the walls—likely pieces he found at yard sales. In the middle of the room, a glass coffee table sat between the couches, with a chess board set up and ready for someone to play. In the corner, two pairs of snowshoes were propped next to a fake woodburning stove. I knew that his roommate Marty preferred watching golf to snowshoeing. I wondered for a moment who the second pair belonged to—another one of Dad's mysteries.

We stayed for a whole week and honestly, I fell in love with the little town where he had moved. Despite all the hurt I felt about him moving away from us—after being there, I was better able to understand why he did it. We had good, wholesome fun. And for a week, I almost forgot that we were there because he was dying.

A day after we headed back home, Dad sent an email to our whole family, inviting us back the following summer. He was proud of what he had built, and he had hopes of being around for another year.

24

UNLIMITED LOVE

Amidst the chaos of Dad's sickness, and the constant feeling that the other shoe was about to drop, my life continued to march on. I was trying so hard to avoid breaking down that I had made it near impossible to feel *anything*. I was numb, living on autopilot. It was hard for me to feel joy or excitement about anything. I simply suited up and showed up, as Dad had taught me.

Our ninth-year wedding anniversary was at the end of the summer, and I decided to surprise Rob with tickets to see the Red Hot Chili Peppers in Los Angeles. Like every other person over thirty-five, I was familiar with all their classic songs—Under the Bridge, Otherside, Scar Tissue, Californication, to name a few. I had always loved the classics, but I was not a die-hard fan by any stretch of the imagination. In fact, if you had asked me to name one Red Hot Chili Pepper band member, I'd fail. But they had just released a new album, and my husband had been introducing me to some new songs over the last few weeks, so I thought it would be a fun thing to try.

In the weeks leading up to the concert, I was trying to force myself into feeling excited about it. I had secured a babysitter so we could get away for a whole night—stay at a hotel without the kids. A real night away as grown-ups!

The day of the concert, we drove down to Manhattan Beach to check into our hotel. I was miffed when I saw a picture of the place Rob booked for us—it looked like a glorified Super 8 in the pictures on Yelp. It wasn't exactly giving "romantic night away" vibes. I was grumpy, and I could feel myself ruining the mood. I tried to fight hard against it. To will a better mood to come to me. Eventually, it worked.

The hotel wasn't as bad as the pictures made it look. We had sushi together at a boutique local joint and I managed not to spill soy sauce on my new white bodysuit.

As we walked up to SoFi Stadium a few hours later, I could feel the excitement starting to grow. Thousands of people in Chili Pepper gear flooded the stadium parking lot. We climbed higher and higher and *higher* up the stadium stairs.

"You are so your dad," Rob muttered between short breaths. I refused to take the escalator even though we were sitting in the nosebleeds.

When the band finally took the stage, what happened next shocked me. Over the next two hours, I completely lost myself. We were so far away from the stage that the man in the seat next to me had to use binoculars to see the band. But the distance didn't matter to me, because the music traveled from that stage straight to my soul. Bass lines bumped through my chest, and the singer's voice flittered through my ears and swirled around my head, igniting a lightness within me that I had not felt in years—if ever. In those two hours, I forgot all about Dad and his cancer, I forgot about potty-training and goldfish crackers and feeding the dogs and calling the clients and doing the work. I forgot it all and just *existed*.

I didn't feel numb, I felt *alive*, and that feeling hit me like the very first high of a drug addict. "Ahhhhhhhhhhh!" my soul said with a sweeping exhale. "You *are* capable of feeling pure happiness."

After that concert, I did everything to try and capture that feeling again. I listened to the Red Hot Chili Peppers every single day. Forget the classics, I scoured the internet for their original songs from the 1980s. I listened to every album from start to finish. I read all the lyrics. I read fan websites to learn about the meaning behind all the songs. I was constantly searching for more.

It didn't matter that the band had been in existence for forty years—this level of adoration was new to me, and it was what kept me afloat as I battled Dad's decline.

My family began to poke fun at me for being a super-fan and for having a crush on Anthony Kiedis (yes, I did eventually learn the lead singer's name, along with the names of everyone else in the band and all the former members who had come and gone).

But it was more than that. I wasn't a crazed teen with a weird infatuation. I was a grown woman who had been living in an unrelenting state of fight-or-flight, and their concert had finally given me a glimpse of true peace and happiness, and I wanted to cling to it with everything I had.

25

CHEMO SCHEAMO

The chemotherapy was causing Dad's face to swell and blister. By mid-summer, the blisters had begun oozing and his face was literally peeling off in large flakes, leaving him in fear of infection. The doctors told him to stay out of the sun, but he refused. He couldn't help himself—he insisted on continuing to hike. He made do with an umbrella and his bandana around his neck—his "COVID cowboy mask" he joked. But that wasn't enough to protect him. He had always been a handsome man, but the blisters and scabs distorted his face beyond recognition.

Through it all, Dad was obsessed with his bloodwork. For whatever reason, that was the thing that he focused on. But the cancer didn't care about his good bloodwork—it was attacking different parts of his body. He couldn't understand, and in turn, I couldn't either. How *was* the cancer so bad if the bloodwork was so good?

An email from Dad to me and his doctor:

From *Father@gmail.com*
To: *daughter@gmail.com; doctor@hospital.net*
Re: *FW: Good day good Doctor. For your review. I know it's*

not good. My bloodwork is perfect and CEA down to 6.3.
Odd case I think? Thanks. Boris Romanowsky
Message: *A picture of Dad's bloodwork.*

His bloodwork was perfect, and so, against the advice of his doctors, he stopped the chemotherapy again. He was reaching out to various other hospitals and clinics to see about alternative therapies and experimental treatments. It was hard to deal with—the constantly changing plans. One minute he was doing chemo, the next he was not. He would go through several rounds of chemo and see improved results on CAT scans, and then he would stop the treatment against the advice of his doctors.

And so, months passed with lots of back and forth, ups and downs and all arounds. My mood was inextricably tied to the status of his cancer, and I didn't know how to unentangle it. If he got a good scan, I would feel relieved. If he got a bad scan, I was sad. And in between all of that, I was on eggshells waiting for the next bit of bad news.

The next bad news came in February 2023.

THE EXPERIMENTAL TREATMENTS and researchers all denied taking Dad's case. He was running out of options.

By February 2023, Dad had been off chemo and any other treatment for eighty days. As Dad was prone to do, he would text or email bad news. I received a text message one day with a picture of his most recent CAT scan results. The whole page was highlighted and notated by Dad. Large growths everywhere. Perhaps more alarming were the results of his latest blood test. Dad had prided himself on having "good bloodwork" despite everything—but this time, the bloodwork was not good. The numbers were six times what they were supposed to be. His liver panel was literally off the chart.

I had given Dad a lot of leeway in his cancer treatments. I came to appointments when he asked (rarely) and I would listen whenever he wanted to share, but I never told him what to do, or fought with him about what he was doing. But that day, I couldn't help myself—I called his oncologist directly. I needed to know what the hell to think about these numbers.

I finally got through to the doctor and he told me what I suspected: the numbers were very bad news. They were indicative of rapid and aggressive growth of the cancer. In addition, it meant that Dad's liver wasn't functioning properly, and he could die of liver failure before he died of cancer.

I panicked and felt like I needed to get to him immediately. I was supposed to go to Napa that weekend for a work conference. I cancelled it immediately and tried to buy a plane ticket to get to Dad. But when I told him about my plan, he said not to come. He was going skiing in Canada that weekend.

I was gutted. The doctor had just told me that he could die at any moment, and he didn't want me to come? Instead, he was... skiing???

"Fine," I told Dad. "I won't come this weekend, but I am going to come up and see you in two weeks."

MY SISTER and I dropped everything to go and visit Dad in early March. It was clear that his cancer was progressing at a dangerously aggressive level.

Well, I dropped *almost* everything. I had been scheduled to give an in-person work seminar that week. The event was already booked with dozens of people who were planning to come to see me talk.

I didn't want to do it. I didn't care about work or business. I tried to cancel, but I couldn't. The reservations were already made. I was the main speaker. The people were expecting me. The show must go on, or something like that.

We flew to Washington with both our families. The first night, just hours after we arrived, I kicked everyone out of the Airbnb so I could give my presentation via Zoom to dozens of strangers. I dropped everything to go see my dad who was dying, but I didn't forget to pack a suit jacket to put over my tank-top so I could look professional for my Zoom seminar. I spoke to them for an hour and a half about the importance of doing estate planning so their family members could help when they became incapacitated or died. The irony was not lost on me.

I even managed to use the trip as part of the speech—"I can't be with you in person today because I had to fly out of town to visit my father who is dying. But, thanks to his Advanced Health Care Directive, I was able to speak to his doctor directly about his prognosis."

How gross, I thought. *Using my own personal tragedy to get business.* But was I really using it to get business, or was I just speaking the truth? I didn't care about the business; I was being honest. Without that advanced health care directive, I wouldn't have been able to speak to the doctor and I might not have known how bad my dad's condition was. Without it, I would not be in Washington that day.

Dad kept us busy all weekend. He wanted to show us the restaurant at Semiahmoo, his favorite beach walk, his favorite coffee shop in Canada (the border crossing was only five minutes from his house). Really, anything to stay busy and avoid talking to us about anything serious.

Finally, after we had been there for three days, I said, "Dad, we came here to talk to you about your health. We *need* to talk about it. Can we do that this afternoon before we fly home?"

He reluctantly acquiesced.

My girls loved the Airbnb place that we had picked. They called it the "Upside-Down House" because the bedrooms were downstairs and the kitchen and living room were upstairs. It was unintentional, but that house was symbolic of the weekend—everything felt upside-down. Out of order.

That evening, Dad came over to our Upside-Down House. Launa and I sent our families downstairs to go to bed so we could talk to Dad in private. Dad took his shoes off and sat on the couch next to me. Launa sat on the floor. None of us touched. We barely looked at each other.

Dad started talking about his exercise regimen and what he was doing to prevent the neuropathy in his legs.

Then: "So, what did my doctor tell you?" The quick topic switch was jarring.

Just like when he gave us the sticky note about his insurance, he was coming at us like we had overstepped. Like we didn't have a right to know what was going on with him and his health.

"Well, he said that you could die of liver failure any day..." I started as the tears poured out.

Dad got agitated. "I don't think my doctor believes me when I tell him that I did 1,000 reps of leg press this weekend. I pressed 1,200 pounds in one hour. Maybe that was a little too much. My legs are fine—super strong—and the neuropathy is better, so I switched to jumping rope again! Does that sound like someone who is going to drop dead?"

He was right. It *didn't* make sense. But the numbers and the CAT scans didn't lie, either, and he knew that—he just didn't want to acknowledge it.

But somehow, his heart softened a little bit, and he began to talk about "the end." Where he wanted to go for hospice. Where he wanted to be buried. What he wanted us to do with the house. What he wanted us to do with his personal things.

I had been so frustrated with him for avoiding this hard

conversation all weekend, but now that we were having it, I wanted it to stop. I didn't want to be discussing these things at all.

I couldn't look at him. I was trying so hard to hold it together for him. To be brave and stoic like I always was. As the tears rushed down my face, all I could focus on were his feet. He sat on the couch with his long legs outstretched and his feet crossed at the ankles. I didn't realize it then, but his pressed dark jeans were hiding how thin his legs were becoming. His large feet were encased in thick wool socks and as he talked, he rubbed them back and forth, back and forth. It was as though, even as he sat reclined on the couch in this Upside-Down house, he was itching to move. To run. To keep going. Not to stop. The emotional walls were so close to crashing down. There, in that Upside-Down house.

THE SECOND THE plane touched down in Los Angeles, I broke out in tears. Not just tears—sobs. Body-shaking sobs. I was in the middle of a crowded plane with my young children, and I was feeling the most intense sorrow of my life. I had to stuff my sweatshirt into my mouth and bite down to try and physically stop the sobs from erupting out of my throat.

In that moment, all of my emotional walls evaporated, and I was consumed by fear that I may never see my dad alive again.

26

A VERY UN-MERRY BIRTHDAY

I did see Dad alive again. In May, he decided to travel back to California for a visit the week of his birthday.

We planned to go to dinner at Brophy Brother's in the harbor on the date of his actual birthday. Over the months leading up to his birthday, Dad mentioned several times how incredible it was that he was turning 65—an age many of his brothers never saw. I was hoping we could celebrate his birthday and talk to him about the current situation, his CAT scan results and his plan for the near future. My sister, her family, and another cousin came up from San Diego just to see him.

But when we arrived at the restaurant, we found Dad seated at a large table with a beautiful woman, a young man with sunglasses on, and a large Bernese Mountain dog. We had never seen these people or their dog in our lives. Wine glasses littered the table.

"What the fuck..." Launa whispered under her breath.

As we walked tentatively to the dinner table, Dad looked at us and jumped up from his chair. "Oh hello!" he said with a mild slur. "This is my friend from high school! She just happened to be in town, and I told her and her son to come join us for dinner!"

The woman looked mortified. "Well, actually, your dad invited me for dinner, but he didn't tell me that it was his birthday or that his whole family was coming. I can leave."

"Oh no, no, no. You stay! We will all stay and enjoy each other!" Dad boasted as he pointed to the open chairs.

In that moment, the only person enjoying themselves was Dad.

My sister and I fumed. We hadn't seen Dad since we left Washington in March, with his future uncertain. He just received a horrible health diagnosis, and now he was here, back in California, and we couldn't talk to him about it because he invited some random friend from high school to dinner.

This was no accident. It was very calculated. Dad would go to any lengths to avoid having difficult conversations—including inviting random dinner guests to join us so he knew that we wouldn't dare bring anything up.

He was right. We didn't. It was an incredibly uncomfortable dinner. He was clearly buzzed from the wine and enjoying the high school flashbacks with this woman. The rest of us sat at the end of the table muttering to ourselves, bothered about the whole situation.

The only thing that got me through the dinner was remembering that Dad was in town for several days, and there would be other opportunities to talk to him about his health and the recent CAT scan.

But as it turns out, that wasn't true either. We barely saw Dad again on that trip. We tried to meet up with him multiple times, but our schedules didn't align. Though he was in California for five days, he packed each day full of various events with different people.

Once again, I was angry, sad, and confused. Why did he come all the way to California just to see us for a few hours? Who else was he even seeing? What was he doing? I didn't learn all the answers until after he died, and I looked at his day timer. He was going to the gym, attending art walks and visiting his old cub scout leader from elementary school. Not his kids. Not his grandkids. According to his doctor, his days were numbered. And this is how he was spending them?

———

I HAD BEEN SUFFERING from serious sinus problems for the last few years and needed to have surgery. But for the last two years, I had repeatedly rescheduled the surgery and put off my own treatment because I had been so overwhelmed with obsessively worrying about Dad and *his* health.

The next Cousin's Day Fourth of July event at Dad's was just a few weeks away, but after the Brophy Brother's incident in May, I was furious with him. I didn't want to spend money to fly my whole family to visit him in Washington when he barely visited me when he was in town in May. I didn't want to abide by his rules anymore. I was sick of his shenanigans and his yanking us around all the time with no repercussions.

But I was too chicken-shit to tell him that. So instead, I created a false conflict. I rescheduled my sinus surgery for the week of the Fourth of July and emailed him to tell him I couldn't go because of my medical procedure.

Take that, I thought. *I am taking care of me! Screw you and your dumb house that you bought so far away!*

But the truth is, I never felt good about doing this. I was trying to solve a problem without just addressing the issue head-on—that my feelings were hurt that he didn't want to see us more. That I was scared to lose him.

Dad emailed me a few days later:

To: daughter@gmail.com
From: Father@gmail.com
Re: Cousin's Day
Message: Ok Boomer, it's important to take care of your

medical care and you've been having sinus issues for a while now. I was just planning on having this as the last Cousin's Day in Washington. Let's see what my latest CAT scan says. I am sure can make it to the 4th of July... after the 4th... we will see what happens.

Sometimes, the universe does for us that which we cannot do for ourselves. Despite my efforts to reschedule the surgery and manufacture a conflict to avoid having a difficult conversation with my dad about my feelings, I would not be having my surgery after all. I received a call from my doctor's office—my insurance was refusing to approve the procedure, even though they had previously authorized it. My doctor would have to appeal the decision. It would take weeks, if not months, to sort it out.

That same week, Dad received the latest CAT scan, which showed aggressive growth even since May.

Okay, fine, Universe, I thought. *You win. I am going to Washington again.*

27

BASECAMP BLAINE

From the second we landed in Washington on July 2, Dad started barking orders at us. We had arrived at the airport at the same time as three of his other friends, and he had elaborate plans about which rental cars each of us were going to use and where we were going to go. It's amazing, really, how one man single-handedly directed seven grown adults. None of us stood up to him, even when his plans weren't really making sense. Even as his health continued to deteriorate, he still held such an aura of authority. People just listened to him.

Back in May, I had wanted to spend as much time as possible with Dad while he was in California. Now that I was up in Washington, it was hard for me to spend any time with Dad. He was on edge, and I was too. I could tell that he was declining, although he put on a hell of a show to try and hide it.

Dad always had a knack for turning any regular event into an exercise. At one point, he challenged my sixteen-year-old cousin to a stick battle. Each of them held onto the outer edges of a long piece of wood. They each pushed and shoved, exerting massive amounts of upper body strength trying to force the stick away from themselves and onto the other person. Nobody would ever guess that stick-fighting man was sick. But I could tell. He didn't battle as long as normal. And more shocking to those close to him—he sat down and rested after.

Cousin's Day was our version of a family reunion. The relationships among my dad and all his living siblings were distant, but somehow the next generation—their children—had started to bond. Dad was the only one of his generation who usually came to Cousin's Day, and over the years, he had developed a habit of always inviting one random non-cousin to Cousin's Day. But this year, there was no denying that things were different. He had not invited just *one* random person. No, in addition to all the cousins, he had also invited several of his childhood friends. It was clear to me that he was intending this to be a goodbye party.

Of the friends, there was one woman in particular who struck me—Anita. After my parents divorced, Dad had a string of girlfriends, but Anita was the first and the most serious. She was also the most confusing to me, because Dad kept her the most secret. Hers was the face in that picture on the refrigerator on that fateful first Thanksgiving after the divorce. The one we met over chips and salsa at the Mexican restaurant while Dad was counting cars entering the parking lot. Dad was never able to just be honest and tell us he was seeing her. We wouldn't have cared—it's not like we blamed her for their divorce. Our parents' marriage was over long before Anita came around—in practicality, if not legally.

But Dad could never just admit to us that she was his girlfriend and that he loved her.

Anita was always a mysterious figure in the shadows. Someone who appeared to be important to my dad, but who he couldn't fully integrate into our lives. And so, for those years they were together—even living together—we knew little about her and spent little time together with the two of them. When they broke up in 2009, he was devastated. He got drunk and cried to my husband about it. For weeks, he rode his bike for hundreds of miles at nighttime to try and exercise the pain away.

And yet here she was, fifteen years later, at our Cousin's Day event in Washington.

They sat close to each other and spoke in whispers. Dad, always the awkward one, said to me, "You remember Anita, right?"

How could I forget? Still, an air of secrecy surrounded everything he did. They were clearly more than friends again.

The week was beautiful, but truth be told, I barely spent any time directly with Dad. He was clearly on edge—when he wasn't stick-fighting young cousins, he was obsessively cleaning, muttering about people making his house dirty, and directing people where to go and what to do. (Artists Point Trailhead! Vancouver! Marty's Diner!)

At first, I was angry that he was so cranky. We had all flown thousands of miles and spent thousands of dollars to come and visit him. A trip that he had insisted we all make. And now he was going to be rude and cranky about our kids spilling some crumbs in his house? But as time went on that week, my heart began to soften as I tried to imagine what he must be feeling. What must it be like to host a party with your friends and family, knowing it may be the last one you ever attend? Knowing that you might not see some of these people ever again? I couldn't imagine the pain and anguish that would cause.

Once I realized that, I was no longer angry. I just felt a deep sorrow for him—and for us. We were all hurting and trying to pretend like we weren't. But the pretending was getting harder and harder. I knew that despite his cantankerous mood, somewhere deep down he felt joy and pride when he looked out across his huge green lawn and saw the next generations laughing and playing. And so, I made it my personal mission to have as much fun as possible with my family that week, since that was the way I knew how to show Dad love.

As my children climbed trees in fairy wings and ate so many chips their bellies hurt, I knew that we were giving Dad his true bucket-list item: a safe and happy family.

PART IV

BACK TO THE BEGINNING

28

BONZI TRIP

Growing up, any time our dad wanted to make an emergency trip, he'd call it a "Bonzi Trip." To us, a "Bonzi Trip" meant to travel somewhere at the last minute. Quickly and with minimal planning and very few supplies.

Dad was always in charge of the Bonzi Trips—but now, it was me and Launa who were making the Bonzi to go save Dad.

After Dad called that Thursday, I left at 4 a.m. on Friday morning to drive to Burbank airport and catch a flight to Bellingham, Washington. I would arrive around 11a.m. and Launa would arrive around 2 p.m. since she was on a different flight from San Diego. Dad would pick us up.

I got to the airport early and dropped my car at the valet. I realized that I had no plan for picking my car back up—I hadn't thought that far ahead. My sole mission was to make it to Blaine and get Dad. I'd figure out the car pick-up later.

I entered the airport and was shocked at how quiet and quaint it was. Historically, we flew out of the urban hellscape that is LAX; this was a breath of fresh air.

Since I was full of nervous energy, I racked up almost 6,000 steps before boarding my 7 a.m. flight. Right as we boarded, I texted my friend from college, Bridgette. By some divine coincidence, Bridgette and her family had moved from Salt Lake City to Bellingham just three short weeks earlier. I had not seen Bridgette since her wedding eight years earlier, but I reached out to let her know I was coming and would be in Bellingham by 11 a.m. Miraculously, Bridgette's schedule was free, and she agreed to pick me up from the airport.

I arrived in Bellingham with just a backpack and a small tote bag. After a few minutes, Bridgette drove up to the pickup in her black Nissan. In that moment, it seemed like no time had passed at all since we had last seen each other. I was so relieved. Despite not seeing each other for years, we instantly fell back into easy communication.

We spent the next four hours catching up and talking about motherhood. How difficult it was for us emotionally, as introverts, to raise children. Why were they always talking? Why were they always touching us? But we also shared the fun parts – watching our children learn new things and mispronounce words. As we chatted, we hiked together through the winding trails behind her house. The lush trees provided us with a cool shade, and I found my mind wandering, imagining my family here with hers in this little town by the trees. In my fantasy world, we'd live nearby and hike this trail every day. But I knew that would not be reality. Even if we did move to Bellingham, our lives would be so busy with our own schedules that we probably wouldn't see each other much anyway.

Eventually, I had to rip myself away from the nostalgia and face the reality of why I was there: to pick up my dying father and bring him home to California.

On the way back to the airport, I received a text from Dad's friend and roommate, Marty: *I just pulled into the waiting area.*

A wave of nausea overcame me. Dad always came to the airport to greet us, even when we had rental cars and didn't need him to come. He was always there, waiting for us the second we got off the airplane. The fact that he had sent Marty to get us was immediately alarming.

Bridgette dropped me off, and Launa and I hopped into Marty's blue four-door truck. His somber mood didn't match the sunny weather outside.

"Your dad is resting and so he sent me to get you," Marty began.

We all knew the real meaning behind this sentence—Dad was declining, and fast. Dad never rested. He would never send someone else to get us from the airport. He *couldn't* get us, and that thought made me sick.

"How is he really doing, Marty?" I asked.

"Well," Marty began in his slow and quiet voice. "He has been sleeping a lot, which you know he never does. I am worried about him."

I am sure we spoke more on the drive, but that's all I can recall. The rest was a blur.

We pulled up to the house twenty minutes later. At first glance, it appeared that Dad was waiting for us in the yard, leaning against the wooden fence that surrounded his large lawn. But it was only Manny—the life-sized mannequin that Dad bought from a clothing store that was going out of business. To confuse his neighbors, Dad would dress Manny in his clothes and move him around the yard. It was still summer, so Manny was wearing jeans, a light shirt and a sunhat.

As we pulled into the long gravel driveway, I looked over at the sign that Dad had put up at the end of the driveway: "Basecamp Blaine" in blue lettering on wood. Dad was so proud of this place, and his personality was written all over it.

We got out of Marty's truck and quietly entered the house through the back sliding door into the huge open room. I don't even know what to call it – a living room? It had concrete floors, a huge sectional couch, and a podcast station in the corner with a few unplugged microphones. Dad had likely never listened to a podcast, let alone recorded one. Why he needed a podcast station in his house was anybody's guess.

My breath caught in my chest. My father was curled up in a fetal position in a dimly lit corner of the living room. He was fully dressed, in jeans and a T-shirt, lying on top of the bed. The bits of his skin that were showing were pale gray and cracking. He repeatedly rubbed his feet together—just like he had when we came to visit in March and talked about the end. He said he did it to help with the blood flow and to counteract neuropathy, but I knew it was also a sign of his anxiety.

He wore no socks, and his feet were so thin I could see the bones protruding. His skin stretched tight, wrapping over his bones like cellophane over leftover food.

"Girls, is that you?" he muttered without opening his eyes.

"Yes, Dad, we're here," Launa squeaked out—likely suffering the same shock that I was.

"I am just resting here for a bit," Dad lied, as if we couldn't see for ourselves that he was morphing into a shell of himself. "Why don't you girls go down to the bar for dinner? Get some shrimp and rice. Take Marty with you."

Even in his weakest moments, he could still maintain control by directing us. We didn't want to go to dinner with Marty—we wanted to go by ourselves and strategize. And yet, minutes later, we loaded back in the car and found ourselves driving to the bay with Marty.

My sister and I are both strong, fiercely independent women, and yet we still could not stand up to our dad even when he was in the fetal position with his eyes closed.

THE NEXT MORNING, Dad woke us up at 5:30 a.m. to start driving. Miraculously, he was standing in the kitchen sipping a coffee.

"I told you I was just resting!" he insisted. "We better hit the road. We will switch every ninety minutes, which is approximately every hundred miles. Keep our bodies moving and our blood flowing. No tired drivers! I'll drive the first leg. Hop in."

Launa and I climbed into the car as directed, but not without apprehension. He was going to drive?

I don't remember much of the first leg, to be honest. I was mostly focused on looking at Dad to make sure he was coherent and not overmedicated.

After that first leg (not a mile over 100), Dad took some painkillers and then said he was done for the rest of the drive, and it was up to Launa and me to finish from there.

Launa and I drove down I-5 for the next twenty-three hours straight, switching drivers every hundred miles like clockwork. The entire drive, we never turned the music on once. The three of us just talked. Dad sat in the back and peeked his head between the two front seats—talking the whole entire drive in his booming voice and ensuring there was no way either of us would fall asleep.

I will never forget that drive. Everything about it was classic Dad. From the fact that we didn't listen to any music, to the way he directed us what to do from the backseat, to the wild stories he told.

We had arrived back in Ventura at 5 a.m. that Sunday morning, after traveling for nearly twenty-four hours straight. When we pulled up to my house, all I wanted to do was go inside and crash into my own bed. But Dad insisted on "getting settled" before going to bed. So, at 5 a.m., we completely unloaded the car and organized his things in his new temporary bedroom—my home office.

In the years since my parents divorced, my dad had resettled many times: Montecito, Santa Barbara, Tahoe, and finally Washington. I didn't know then that my home office would be his final resettlement.

29

NEW PLANS

"I heard a bunch of screaming this morning and I panicked! I thought for sure the car was careening off the I-5 and we were headed to sudden death!" Dad greeted me as he walked downstairs. "Then I woke up and realized it was just your children fighting over the TV remote!"

Dad always did have a wry sense of humor.

In those first few days of Dad being at our house, I found myself in a permanent state of uncertainty. I knew how serious the situation was, and yet I also had a hard time believing it. Maybe it *wasn't* really that bad?

Dad was having a hard time believing it, too. Dr. Lambert in Washington had told him that without chemo and with rapid growth, his days were numbered. When he got back to Ventura, I wanted to help make him comfortable and encourage him to visit with people. But that was not what he wanted. He insisted on not seeing or talking to any friends until he met with Dr. Anderson.

Dr. Anderson had not been involved in any of Dad's treatment and hadn't been his doctor in at least fifteen years.

Yet, for the next forty-eight hours, nothing mattered to Dad except getting to see Dr. Anderson.

"What do you want me to tell all the cousins, Dad? How much information do you want me to share?"

"Well, we can't tell them anything until I see Dr. Anderson, because we don't have any new information, right?"

I was frustrated—what was Dr. Anderson going to tell him that Dr. Lambert hadn't told him just last week? The cancer was widespread, he had no more treatment options, and his days were numbered. But Dad trusted Dr. Anderson and notwithstanding the fact that he hadn't seen him in fifteen years, he wanted to hear *his* opinion. He trusted Dr. Anderson to tell it to him straight.

The appointment with Dr. Anderson was scheduled for Monday, the day after we arrived in Ventura. But due to a sudden surgery, it got pushed back to Thursday. Those seventy-two hours between the anticipated appointment and the actual appointment felt like a thousand.

For the past two-and-a-half years, Dad never took any pain medicine other than Ibuprofen. It wasn't until that week when we picked him up from Washington that he finally started to take the pain meds. Once he started, he became obsessed. He would report to us every time he took them, and then he would jot it down in his day planner. He was worried about becoming addicted and so in between the Norco, when his stomach started to hurt, he took Tums. TUMS. The man was in the end stages of colon cancer, and he thought *Tums* would help alleviate his symptoms. He should have reached out to them for sponsorship—he had a lot of faith in those fluorescent, chalk-covered, over-the-counter antacids.

Some days, we spent hours at my kitchen table together, making phone calls to his health insurance and his retirement to confirm his benefits and beneficiaries. He was trying hard to be productive, but I could tell he was getting confused from the pain meds. Making these phone calls made him feel confident and in control. Later, he beamed with pride as he relayed to Rob how productive we had been.

In the evenings, we gradually got into a routine. Dad would lay down and rest in his room while Rob and I completed our routine of dinner, bath, and bedtime with the girls. Once the girls were asleep, I would get Dad out of his room, and we would watch an episode or two of *Justified*.

Justified was the story of a trigger-happy U.S. marshal, who was banished to Kentucky after a few too many on-the-job "incidents" in Florida. The story followed his return to rural Kentucky and his attempt to avoid getting sucked back into the underbelly of his upbringing. Dad loved it.

Sitting and watching TV together at night brought me simultaneous joy and sorrow. It was nice to sit and just be together. Of course, since the show was about a U.S. marshal, Dad had to offer his input the whole way: "A real U.S. marshal would never wear a *brown* belt with a *black* badge—that's how you know no real law enforcement officers were consulted for this show!" But as we watched episode after episode each night, a heaviness was always present in the air. For Dad to be sitting still for this long meant he was entering into the final stages of his life. He tried to play it off as just "resting," but I knew that he was incapable of voluntarily resting his mind or his body—this was a forced slow-down by Mother Nature.

The appointment with Dr. Anderson finally came. I tried to bravely hold in my emotions, but my tears betrayed me, streaming down my face the second we started walking toward the back room. The office décor remained unchanged from the 1990s, when we would visit for my yearly childhood checkups. I stared straight ahead at the familiar photograph of the dirty-soled ballet shoes and tried not to blink. I tried to will the tears away by force of mental strength—and failed.

Of course, Dr. Anderson had no new information, no news to give us that we hadn't already heard.

"The cancer metastasized all over your body and is not

responding to treatment anymore. It will eventually cause your organs to shut down. You could die tomorrow, or you could die in a few months—we just don't know."

We spoke with Dr. Anderson for several more minutes about end of life information, POLST forms and hospice orders, before the doctor asked, in closing, "Do you have any questions?"

Dad pulled out his pen and methodically asked each question he had written down on his yellow pad attached to his trusty clipboard. As he went through each question, he checked them off with a pen.

"How are your daughters?"

"They're good, thanks for asking."

"Are they still playing softball?"

"No, they're in their forties now!"

"Should I go on hospice?"

"Maybe. You definitely qualify, but if it were me, I wouldn't want nurses checking in on me every few days. But it's up to you."

"Is it true that the hearing is the last sense to go?"

"I don't know—I have never asked a dead person."

That last answer was an attempt at humor, I know, but it wounded me to hear the doctor say it. Dad was scared. He wanted to know what was coming next. I was angry at the doctor for making light of his question—it felt belittling.

I was also angry at Dr. Anderson for not encouraging Dad to go on hospice. I am not a doctor, but telling Dad that he might make it for a few more months seemed completely unreasonable.

With no new information, Dr. Anderson sent us on our way. I felt more confused than before; but Dad felt like we had a plan.

The next morning, I woke up to get the girls ready for school. Dad's bed was made, but he was gone. These disappearing acts happened multiple times over the next few weeks.

He would get up at 4 a.m. and drive to the Santa Monica

mountains by himself to go hike before the sun came up. By this time, he had whittled down to a wiry 177 pounds and was barely eating. Yet he still found the strength and willpower to go to his favorite places and exercise. He was determined to suck every ounce of life out of this world before he left it.

30

COMA BOY

On August 6, 2023, I went on my last hike with my dad at Point Dume, Malibu. Slowly, he trudged to the top of the hill, my family and I following behind. As always, he walked ten paces ahead of us. He held his teal umbrella above his head and his black nylon pants *swished* with each step he took. Somehow, on this day, my children knew not to complain about the difficulty of the hike.

By the time the kids and Rob and I arrived at the top of the rock, Dad was already sitting alone, his umbrella discarded to the side. He sat with his back to us and stared out at the California coast. He was in the direct sunlight. Exposed. But he didn't care.

He stared down at the beach where he had spent his childhood summers outdoors. The beach where he had taken his own children to play in the waves. The beach where, decades earlier, the same sun had bleached his hair blonde and bronzed his scratched and bruised body. The beach where he had been able to escape from his hellish childhood home.

As dad faced north, a gust of wind blew from the south, forcing his hair into a harsh part in the back of his head—the blonde long since faded to brown, the brown recently overtaken by grays.

Dad's last hike

My kids *oooohed* and *ahhhhed* over the view of the ocean, but dad was silent.

Five short minutes later, he stood up and, without saying anything, started the descent.

Overhead, a gull screeched. The violent screech matched the guttural scream bubbling inside my throat. But I put on a brave face, swallowed my scream, and followed my dad down our last mountain.

AFTER DAD PASSED, I looked in his Day-Timer to find that almost every day of the last month of his life was laid out in his calendar.

> *August 2: Robbie home from work, Carpinteria Beach walk, El Pollo Loco for dinner. August 3: Jump rope at Zuma Rock, pick up Norco, go to dry cleaners.*

All those mornings we woke up and found him missing were filled with solo hikes and beach walks, coffee with "the guys at Peets," and more. Dad was always a lone ranger—a man who did his own thing, on his own time and on his own terms. I should have known that was how the end would be, and yet it still shocked me.

It also shocked my nervous system. By that time, I was barely working a few hours a day, just to keep things afloat. Although Dad had not yet formally started hospice, I still referred to him as being "on hospice" because that was easier for people to understand. But sometimes I felt like a fraud. Was Dad really dying if he was running around town and hiking on his own? In my gut, I knew that he was—I could see him turning more jaundiced every day, and his already-loose clothes started to get looser. My eyes could see it, my heart could feel it, but my brain just couldn't logically process how those two things could be true at the same time—he could be near death *and* still hiking. For any normal person, this seems unimaginable. But Dad was never normal.

Thanks to Dad's detailed notes, I now know that in the three weeks before he passed, he went hiking to Zuma Rock at least four times. He walked on Carpinteria Beach at least twice. He went to Peet's Coffee almost daily. He went to bookstores and the dry cleaner. He moved until he could no longer move; wrote until he could no longer write.

And then? We did those things for him.

AFTER THE APPOINTMENT with Dr. Anderson, we found ourselves in a state of flux. We knew Dad was dying, and Dad knew he was dying—and yet he still was not ready for us to call hospice.

In his mind, Dad had a great plan. He would stay at my house until it was near "the end" and then he would go to Sarah House in Santa Barbara for his final days. In the 1990s, Sarah House was a low-income clinic for AIDS patients. Dad was familiar with it because he had sent some of his "guys" (a.k.a. his parolees) there. According to Dad, the staff at Sarah House was kind and compassionate and the place was beautiful. He wanted to spend his final days there.

He told us ad nauseum that because he was retired from the State of California, he had "top-notch" insurance though CalPERS and CCPOA, which would cover his final days. I am an estate planning attorney. I have practiced in this area of law for ten years. In the back of my mind, I knew that long-term care insurance, not basic health insurance, is what covers these types of stays. I also knew that Dad didn't have long-term care insurance. But, despite everything I knew about Dad, and everything I knew about the law, I chose to believe him. I believed that he had investigated this plan to spend his final days at Sarah House. Turns out, I was wrong.

Sarah House does take end-of-life patients for hospice care, but the facility is not covered by insurance. It is a private-pay facility, the cost of which is a sliding scale based on a person's income. The hospice is fully covered by Medicare—but the actual cost of living in the facility is not.

We felt that Dad was at "the end" and that if he wanted to go to Sarah House, now was the time. But he didn't think so. He thought he should stay put at my house for the time being.

If he was going to stay put, then he needed to have nurses coming to my house to check on him. I asked him daily if we could call hospice to get them to at least come to the house and talk to us about our options. For a while, he was adamantly against it. Eventually, Launa coordinated for hospice to come and do an intake on Tuesday, August 15 and Dad agreed.

On Sunday, August 13, Dad told us he wanted to go out to breakfast. The invitation was an interesting proposition, given that he was barely able to eat at that point. Nevertheless, we agreed to go.

As we sat at the table at Two Trees Café that morning, I couldn't focus. Everyone's voices sounded like the mom in the old Charlie Brown cartoons: "Wah wah, wah wah, wah wah." The kids scribbled with crayons, my seven-month-old nephew banged his silverware on the table, and I tried to choke back tears. I willed myself not to listen to the music that was playing, because almost surely it would make me cry. Instead, I stared at the table and tried to act interested in the scribbles the girls were making on their napkins. I knew in my gut that would be the last time we ever had a meal out with Dad.

Although we had planned to meet for breakfast at 8 a.m., Dad had left the house at 7 a.m. and said he would meet us there, even though the restaurant was only three blocks away. Because he arrived an hour earlier than we had planned, he already had a full plate of food in front of him by the time we got there. He had eaten only watermelon and coffee for the last few days, but he somehow managed to choke down some scrambled eggs while we were there.

As soon as our food came, Dad decided he was ready to go. He had eaten already, after all.

"You guys take your time and enjoy your meal—I am going to head home to rest."

As he stood up to leave, he added, "By the way, can you call to see if hospice can come out today instead of Tuesday?" Then he left, the glass door swinging shut behind him.

I almost choked on my sourdough. He had been adamantly against hospice for days, and now he wanted them to come sooner? Of course, he dropped this bombshell on us in the middle of a public breakfast place. In doing so, he left us no time for questions, no time to process. Just instructions—get it done.

And so, we did.

Before my sister left the restaurant to go put her son down for a nap, she called hospice and arranged for someone to meet me at my house.

A social worker arrived at my house just one hour later. A tiny Latina woman with shoulder-length brown hair and an unassuming face, she came armed with her pamphlet of paperwork and walked straight into the lion's den.

What happened next was one of the most painful moments of the last weeks of Dad's life—which is saying a lot, given what was to come.

The woman had barely pulled her chair up to the table when Dad launched into his diatribe:

"The doctors already offered me the traditional treatment when I was diagnosed thirty-two months ago, and I would have been in a damn coma by now had I done the traditional method. It's now getting to a point where I am starting to feel the pain, and that's why you're here."

"Ok, sir."

"No!" he cut her off. "I am trying to present my case. I don't think you've read a file on me. I have done this before—I cared for my brother in Lompoc, my brother in Agua Dulce, my mother. I have seen the ugly side of cancer, and I am trying to tell you—this isn't my first rodeo."

"Sir, I am just trying to explain to you what you can do with home health and what you can do with hospice. It is your choice. With home health, the nurse comes, takes your vital signs and reports to the doctor—"

"But that's not your company? You're hospice?"

"No, sir, we have home health, palliative care and hospice with our company."

"Well, I am at the lowest level right now—home health. Let's stick with the home health care for treatment."

"But Dad—" I interjected through tears. "You don't need home health; you aren't doing treatment anymore. You need hospice."

"I can still treat myself through this!" Dad held up a bottle of Norco and shook it aggressively, the pills rattling.

"Sir," the social worker tentatively cut in, "that's not treatment, that is pain management. Home health is where someone comes and takes you to the doctor, takes you to get x-rays, drives you to your chemotherapy appointments. If you aren't doing any of that anymore, you need hospice."

"All I wanted to do as a transitional phase of my demise is to stay here, stay under the care of my primary physician Dr. Anderson so I can get my anxiety, nausea, vomiting treated as necessary. But stay here—" He pointed his large pointer fingers to the kitchen table and tapped. "—until I become too ill on a day-to-day basis. I don't want to transfer to some random board and care house! Hospice in Santa Barbara will take me thirty, sixty or ninety days out! I have recently been there—the place is gorgeous!"

What Dad wasn't understanding is that nobody—except him—thought he really had thirty, sixty or ninety days left.

When I tried to gently point that out, he became increasingly more hostile. He raised his voice, talked over me and refused to listen to the social worker. He demanded that she give him the address for their facility in Santa Barbara and didn't understand when I told him there was no facility in Santa Barbara.

The social worker didn't understand either, and so she gave him the address for their office building in Santa Barbara. I tried to point out that they weren't talking about the same thing, but neither would listen. Voices escalated, tears fell and finally, the social worker gathered up her unsigned paperwork and practically ran out of the house. Mission: unaccomplished.

I was so despondent, I ran upstairs and locked myself in my room to sob.

Dad went into the garage and found Rob. "They're treating me like an idiot. I know what I am doing. I have seen dozens of people die from cancer. They don't know what they're talking about! I am not going to just lay around this house on hospice like Coma Boy!"

"Boris, she's just trying to help," Rob responded. "You have to be nice to her."

With that, Dad said, "I will be back in three days" and stormed out of the garage.

Nobody knew where he was going or what he was doing. I spent the next hour vacillating between anger, fear, sadness and eventually, acceptance.

I was angry at how Dad treated the hospice social worker. I was embarrassed to have invited this woman into our home, only to have Dad berate her, talk over her, and eventually send her out of the house having accomplished nothing.

I was afraid of where he was, and what he was doing. He had just taken pain medications and should not be driving. What if he got in a car accident on the freeway and killed himself? Or worse, someone else? Where was he going to stay for three days?

I was sad that we had this interaction where we were so angry with each other, and I was pleading with him to just give in and accept his impending death.

And finally, I was in acceptance.

God, grant me the serenity to accept the things I cannot change, the courage to change the things I can, and the wisdom to know the difference.

I was devastated, but I realized that I had no control over my dad, his behaviors, or his emotions. I couldn't control whether he drove his car while on medications and got into a fiery wreck. I couldn't control whether he accepted his rapidly approaching death. I couldn't control how he felt about his condition.

I wanted Dad to accept that he needed hospice, to come to that decision on his own with an open heart and mind. But that just wasn't going to happen, because to him that would mean he had quit, and quitting was never an option for Dad.

I sent Dad a text: *Sorry today went a little sideways. I hope you come back tonight so we can watch the last two episodes of Justified!* My attempt at an olive branch.

That afternoon, Dad came back. He didn't speak to me, tell me where he had been or explain how he felt. He came right into the house and went straight to my office and fell asleep.

At 8:45 p.m. he woke up and acted like nothing had happened. "Are we watching *Justified* tonight or what?" he said in an incensed voice.

And just like that, we fell back into our routine of sitting on the couch together and watching Raylan Givens and his cast of colorful characters.

We stayed up late and watched the season finale of *Justified*. We never watched another show together again.

The next morning, using Dad's Advanced Health Care Directive, I called hospice and signed all the forms for him while he slept.

31

MORPHINE

Once Dad was officially on hospice, time seemed to stand still. Our normal lives were gone, and we were thrown headfirst into the most painful three weeks of my entire life.

I frequently deal with clients who are on hospice, and yet I never knew about the practicalities of the process.

Once hospice is ordered, you are provided with a massive paper bag of medications—lorazepam, morphine, and others. A nurse comes to your house for intake and then leaves you with the patient. After the initial intake, hospice nurses and social workers stop by every few days to check on the person, but unless you pay privately for a separate caretaker, you're in charge of the day to day care and management of your loved one.

When you hear the word "hospice" your mind probably conjures up an image of a frail person. Their breathing labored and slow, their eyes closed, their mind and soul halfway to the other side —wherever that may be. But that could not be further from the truth for us. Like everything else in Dad's life, his "hospice" was far outside the scope of "normal."

The hospice weeks were the hardest weeks of my life. But not because Dad was frail and declining—no, because he fought his imminent death with an unmatched vigor. Dad never gave up. Never admitted defeat. He wasn't ready to go. Watching Dad slowly die reminded me of the caged panthers we drove past on the way to my grandparents' house so long ago, their large and muscular bodies trapped in small metal cages, anxiety radiating off them as they paced back and forth, back and forth.

Thinking about Dad's fight is when my grief hits the hardest. In the end, his death felt like I was helping to take down a rabid animal —one with his back against the wall, teeth bared and snarling, daring us to come closer. Daring us to take him down.

Launa was exhausted from sleeping on our couch for so many days while also trying to care for her infant son and maintain her career as a new Vice Principal. That morning, she drove back down to San Diego to try and prepare for the first week of school and get a little bit of respite. Rob and I were dealing with Dad's hospice on our own for the time being. We set up a hospital-grade bed and the toolbox of medications, but that's where the traditional sense of hospice stopped. Sure, Dad rested more than normal, but he otherwise was totally lucid and talking and even telling jokes.

That Tuesday, we got in touch with Dad's old friend, Sgt. Martin. Dad had worked side-by-side with Sgt. Martin for thirty years, as their law enforcement careers ran parallel to each other. Eventually, their health began to parallel with each other too; Sgt. Martin was diagnosed with colon cancer himself. But Sgt. Martin had another purpose too—a spiritual one. After losing his daughter years earlier, Sgt. Martin left the police department and became a pastor.

In the years since his diagnosis, Dad and I had a lot of hard conversations about his medical care, his finances, his house, and his death. But we never talked about religion. I never asked him what he believed would happen after he died. He obviously knew about the Christian church and its teachings because he raised us in it, but I didn't know if he believed in it himself.

Sgt. Martin came over that afternoon and spent a few hours sitting in Dad's room and talking. As Sgt. Martin was leaving, I grabbed him in the hallway.

"So, did you just sit there and swap old war stories, or did Dad open up at all about... you know." My voice trailed off.

"Oh no, we didn't talk about work much at all," he assured me. "We talked a lot about death and God and heaven, and I think your dad is in a good place. He's a true believer."

I didn't really know how to answer. In recent years, I had a renewed sense of spirituality and had come to trust and believe in a higher power greater than me. It gave me serenity in ways that my old faith had not. I was no longer a "true believer" of the Christian faith that Mom and Dad raised us in. I was glad that Dad had someone that he could open up to about these things, because that person surely was not me.

That night, we left Dad and the girls at home with my mom while Rob and I attended back-to-school night at the preschool. Rob and I sat cross-legged on the grass of the school, eating soggy hotdogs and bags of Doritos with the other preschool parents. We were completely oblivious to the storm that was brewing back home.

At 7 p.m., Rob and I arrived back home, and I instantly sensed that something was wrong. I went to check on Dad. He said that he was in a bit of pain and had just taken a pill—but he never took pills at 7 p.m. Up until that point, his schedule was to take one at 6 p.m., then nap until 8:30, when he'd wake up and we'd watch *Justified*. If he took a pill at 7, that meant that the one he took at 6—just one hour earlier—hadn't done anything to ease his pain.

Turns out, my gut instinct was right—something was very wrong.

Just a few minutes later, Dad started shifting around uncomfortably in bed and began to clear his throat repeatedly.

"Hey, Sasha Boom..." he started. "Did those nurses, um, give you anything stronger than those pills? Maybe some morphine."

My heart stopped. Of course, I knew Dad would eventually need the morphine; after all, I was the one who had called hospice. I was the one who signed all the paperwork, the one who picked up the medication, the one who sat with the nurse while she explained it all. And yet, I never imagined what the moment would look like when I first had to give my dad the morphine.

I sure didn't imagine it happening twenty minutes after back-to-school night for my four-year-old daughter's preschool.

I walked into the laundry room and over to the light-blue medicine box. With steady hands, I unscrambled the lock and pulled out the bottle of morphine. The powerful drug looked so unassuming in the small white plastic bottle. I eased the plastic syringe into the bottle; a slight "pop" sounded as the syringe slipped back out. I walked over to Dad and squeezed a bit into his mouth while he lay there with his eyes closed.

But the morphine did nothing. Dad immediately asked for more. He writhed in pain as tears welled in his eyes.

"MORE!" he demanded, though gritted teeth and tears.

"MORE" he yelled as he curled into himself.

"MORE!" he screamed as his frail body wrapped around a pillow.

According to the hospice instructions, once we needed to start the morphine, we were to give him one dose every four hours. By then, he had taken four doses in just 30 minutes and was still in excruciating pain.

Rob stepped outside to call the hospice for help.

Back in the office, Dad's panic began to set in. "Call Sgt. Martin back," he barked at me. "Get him to the house, now. I am going to die tonight."

"What...? Dad... no, you are fine, I am giving you the meds. We are calling hospice for help," I stammered.

"This is it. This is the end," he panted. "This is what happened with my brother Vlad. I am going to tell you what is going to happen tonight," Dad instructed through groans of pain.

Even in the last hours of his life, he was directing the show.

"Vlad was in so much pain that night," he continued. "I sat by his bed, and I checked on him every hour. He was dead by 6 a.m. That is what is going to happen. You are going to keep checking on me, and then one time you'll check, and I will be dead." Dad always controlled the narrative—even in death.

Internally, I was screaming. But on the outside, I was calm and collected. All those years of enduring pain, stuffing my feelings, and compartmentalizing made me an expert at handling the most stressful situations in the calmest manner.

"Okay, Dad. Sgt. Martin is on the way. I am going to call Launa and tell her she needs to get back here right away."

As we waited for Sgt. Martin to get back to the house, Dad began to cry. He faced the wall, his frail back aimed at me. Where there once were broad shoulders and tanned muscles, I could now see the sharp outline of rib bones.

"It wasn't supposed to be like this," he murmured through tears. His voice was so quiet, I wasn't sure if he was talking to me or to himself.

"I am not supposed to die. I am supposed to be the cool grandpa. I am supposed to be playing with the grandkids at Basecamp Blaine and taking them on adventures. I am not supposed to die. I am healthy. It isn't supposed to end like this..."

We were never a physically affectionate family. It was never my first or even second instinct to wrap someone in a hug to ease their pain. But in that moment, nature overrode nurture, and I bent over and grabbed Dad's hand and hugged him as tightly as I could.

"I know. I know. None of this is fair," I whispered, not sure if I was talking to him or to myself.

A soft knock on the door.

"Can I come in?" Sgt. Martin's hulking figure emerged through the door for the second time that day.

Relief pulsed through my body. The pastor was here. I had long since left the church of my youth, but I was still comforted by his presence. If Dad died now, at least the pastor was here for us all.

Dad asked for privacy and so I stepped outside and stood alone in the hallway. Mom was upstairs wrangling the kids and attempting to put them to bed, as if this were a normal night. As if a completely chaotic scene were not unfolding downstairs. Thank God she was there to help us with the kids as we dealt with this travesty.

After what felt like an eternity, Sgt. Martin stepped into the hallway. "Your father wants you all here to pray over him. Can you get your husband?"

I walked outside and found Rob. He was across the street, standing in the dark, talking on the phone. The whole day was so traumatic for me that I'd forgotten it could be traumatic for him as well.

"Hey!" I yelled to him through the dark. "HEY! My dad needs us!"

But he didn't come immediately. Instead, he stood across the street, looking up into the sky, fixated like a child who had just learned about the moon.

"GET OVER HERE!" I hollered at him, not caring if I startled our neighbors. I started to walk toward him as I continued. "COME HOME."

I finally caught up to him.

"What the fuck IS that?" he said to me, pointing upward.

I turned and looked up, following his finger toward the black night sky.

It was then that I understood why he couldn't look away. A string of lights clustered together in a curved line, heading toward the deep and empty hole of outer space. Millions of tiny stars were instantly overshadowed by the brilliance of this unnatural string. The pieces moved in unison toward eternity.

"I've never seen anything like that," Rob muttered.

"Maybe it's a sign. Dad's right. He *is* leaving tonight," I whispered.

Together, we stood and stared at the lights in silence. In awe.

The silence was finally punctuated by the voice of Sgt. Martin: "Y'all coming back in?"

We stumbled back into the office where Dad lay with his back to us, staring at the wall. He was barely moving at that point, the morphine having finally kicked in.

Together, we laid our hands on Dad and Sgt. Martin began to pray. I called Launa and put the phone on the speaker so she could hear Dad's last rites with Sgt. Martin while she was driving. Internally, I prayed that she would make it on time before he passed.

I don't remember the rest of the night—maybe I blacked it out of my memory. Did we sit by his bed the whole time? Did we leave the room? At some point, Launa arrived, and Dad was still alive. We sat with him all night.

THE NEXT MORNING, I woke, expecting to find Dad dead, according to his own predictions.

He was still alive, but very catatonic and his breathing was heavily labored. We thought for sure the end was near and began to call all his friends. We offered to hold the phone up to Dad's ear so they could say their goodbyes.

Somewhere along the line, Dad started stirring. We held our breath as we watched him slowly turn to us. And then he opened his eyes and looked around, orienting himself to the room.

"Wow," he murmured. "I am still here? I really thought I was going to die last night!"

Dad didn't die that night, but a part of me did.

That night was the first of many goodbyes over the next two weeks.

32

MIND OVER MATTER

After the first near-death experience, Dad regained a decent amount of strength. He was certainly no longer capable of going on hikes, but he was sitting up and talking and attempting to eat small bits of food. But he knew that he could never get behind the pain again and needed to increase his medications. The Norcos were no longer working, and he needed to stay on a constant string of morphine and lorazepam.

When hospice first started, the nurse conducted an intake interview with Dad where she went over all his symptoms. Though I tried to give them privacy, Dad's booming voice made it impossible for me to *not* overhear at least some of it. The nurse asked him his pain level and he told her one. As in, the lowest pain level possible. The man was certifiably insane.

Before the woman left, I pulled her aside. "I overheard my dad tell you that his pain level was 'one.' I need you to understand that he is the toughest person on earth and never admits pain. A 'one' for Boris is like a 'seven' for every other normal person."

She chuckled, but I was serious. This lack of understanding from the hospice led to some frustrating experiences in the coming days.

The medication doses that hospice had ordered weren't doing enough to keep Dad's pain at bay. By that point, he was taking Norco every three hours with morphine and lorazepam in between, and he was still experiencing pain. After twenty-four hours of meticulously tracking the medications, we had a meeting with the hospice team to discuss our options.

The nurse who was assigned to Dad's case was a short older woman, three weeks away from retirement. Dad could very well be her last patient. After we discussed with her our concerns about Dad's medication and provided her with the medication logs, she called the hospice doctor to discuss it.

"Wow. Oh wow," she repeated into the phone. "Are you sure about those numbers?" she asked the doctor.

She hung up the phone and looked at us. "The doctor wants to start your father on a fentanyl patch for pain and stop the Norco. But I have never seen a doctor prescribe such a high dosage—he wants to start him at 175mcg. Most of my patients get 25 to 50 mcg. This is enough to knock out an elephant..." she trailed off.

Dad allowed us to put the fentanyl patch on his back that day. We took turns sitting in the recliner behind his bed. At one point, several hours later, when it was Launa's turn to watch Dad, I heard panicked yelps from my office. We ran into the room, and we saw her holding up Dad in a bear hug. He was skin and bones, and even though he was wearing the largest fentanyl patch that the nurse had ever seen prescribed, he had insisted on getting out of the bed on his own to go take a shower. But once he stood, he couldn't move—his eyes were glazed over and his feet were cemented to the floor. Launa was singlehandedly holding up all 177 pounds of him against her trembling body.

Dad had always propelled himself through life with a stubborn will, and his hospice was no different.

"Am I in the fast lane or the slow lane to the end?" he said with a faraway look in his eyes as we tried to guide him to the bathroom.

I didn't know how to answer. "Here, let us help you..." I responded as I guided him to the bathroom, where, despite all odds, he insisted on showering by himself.

The prescription fentanyl dosage may have been strong enough to knock out an elephant, but it wasn't enough to knock out Dad.

ONCE WE BROUGHT Dad back to California, he made it clear that he wanted us to keep Anita in the loop about his care. Finally, with Dad stepping back, we were able to have clear and direct communications with her. She came to the house to sit with Dad almost daily. She rubbed his feet, brushed his hair, and talked to him. When Dad was sleeping, she visited us.

In those otherwise painful days, she shared with us beautiful parts of the relationship she and my dad had shared. She showed us photo albums of the two of them on their various adventures. She shared about their travels, their escapades, and their love for each other. It felt real and sincere. It was unexpectedly comforting to sit with her and talk. This woman who, for so long, had been shrouded in mystery. The stories she shared helped me fill in bits of information about those missing years of Dad's life—those years when I was in college and had no idea what he was up to. He was adventuring with Anita. I was happy for him, to have spent these times with her, and to have her here with him in the end.

One afternoon, I noticed a lump on the side of Dad's chest and panicked. "Is the cancer growing so big that it is literally visible to the naked eye?" I wondered out loud.

"No, your dad has always had that small lump on his side," Anita answered. Exposing a level of familiarity with his most intimate self.

Perhaps their relationship didn't work out the way he had

wanted it to, but she was by his side in the end, and that brought me comfort.

———

THE LAST TWO weeks of Dad's life were excruciatingly painful. He vacillated between lucidity and incoherence. Sometimes he would ramble on about seeing things that clearly weren't there. Other times, he would clearly communicate with us about his thoughts.

We received so much conflicting information about the medications during those weeks, it was hard to deal with. There were periods of time where Dad would be incapable of speaking but would twitch and grimace; we interpreted that as his being in pain, while the hospice nurses suggested that perhaps he was just getting antsy about being in bed. "From what you tell us, he's always been physically active, so he's probably just having a hard time laying still," they opined.

But they had no idea the pain he was probably in—physically and mentally. I worried that his moaning and twitching was the emotional pain seeping out of him. That somewhere, inside his brain, he knew he was close to dying and he was fighting it.

We continued to give him increased doses of morphine to try and calm him, but it didn't seem to be working. He continued to groan and twitch. At one point, the hospice nurse panicked at how quickly we were going through the morphine. She went so far as to suggest that perhaps one of Dad's visitors had stolen some doses. "Surely, he isn't taking that much and still moving," she insisted.

I don't know what was worse, the fact that she thought someone had stolen the morphine or the fact that she didn't believe us that Dad really had taken it all and was still in pain.

In addition to worrying about Dad's health, I then began to worry about getting in trouble over the "missing" morphine. I knew without a doubt that we had given it all to Dad. I had no concerns that anybody had stolen any doses or was misusing it. But I had been such a habitual rule-follower all my life that I couldn't stand to think I was somehow going to get in trouble. I was so distraught over it one day that the hospice nurse offered to call my phone and leave me a voicemail telling me I was not in trouble.

"You are not getting in trouble," she said. "You have done nothing wrong."

I still have that voicemail on my phone. Sometimes, when the doubt creeps in, I listen to it to calm my nerves.

Cousins started coming to say their goodbyes. Two decades earlier, Dad had been with them when their fathers died; now, they were here to return the favor. Dad was so heavily medicated by this point that we were taking turns sitting with him bedside. The cousins came to do their shifts.

At one point, after a shift ended, we sat outside on the back patio, doing our best to have conversations notwithstanding the dire circumstances of Dad's condition.

Suddenly—a loud noise. Groaning. Shuffling feet.

A shock—Dad, walking by himself to the backyard to join us.

His shirt hung off his body like a child wearing their father's dress shirt. Pants less, with his bare legs exposed. The flesh on his legs barely stretched over his bones. There was no more muscle. His skin was the color of cantaloupe, aggressively orange in the sunlight, the jaundice proving that his liver had finally stopped functioning.

"I think I will have a cup of coffee," he mumbled before dropping like an anchor into an open seat on the patio. "Hold up my umbrella, won't you?" he directed our cousin.

My sister got him a cup of coffee and my cousin held the umbrella over his head as he took painstaking moves to bring the cup to his lips.

"I guess this is probably my last cup of coffee," he murmured. Then he slowly closed his eyes and turned his face toward the sun—his thin jaundiced neck stretching up toward the sky like a sunflower.

We guided him back to the bed, where he slept the rest of the day.

AUGUST 18, 2023 – a message to everyone via social media:

> Dad continues to astound everyone with his sheer determination and will to live. While he wishes that he could overcome his situation with his usual "mind over matter" approach, his body simply cannot hold out much longer. For those of you who pray, we ask that you pray for him to feel peaceful and secure enough to let go of us here on earth and move on to his next big adventure.

Dad simply refused to go. By the end of the month, he had not eaten or drank for over ten days. We were asking the nurses how long a person could go without food or water, living only on morphine, fentanyl, and mental willpower. Apparently, a long time. They suggested we do things to help ease him into the afterlife: tell him we love him, apologize for anything we had done wrong, tell him we forgive him for anything he had done to us, bring in anybody else who might need to do the same thing.

We agonized over this. We read him poems. We held his hands. We played music. We dusted off an old bible and read it to him. My mom had an opportunity to sit with him, to hold his hand, and to thank him for all the good times they had before their marriage ended; to tell him she would take care of their children and grandchildren when he was gone, to tell him we would be okay.

That our family was able to come together despite everything and provide my dad with these beautiful bedside moments was a testament to the amount of healing that can happen within a family. It was nothing short of a miracle. We shared moments of love, forgiveness, and true beauty in that room.

There were also moments of pure strangeness—like the morning I received a text message from an unfamiliar number. A person who refused to identify himself told me, *If he's still alive, please whisper in his ear that 6 1 4 3 forgives him.*

We told him it was okay to let go. We urged him to let go, we *pleaded* with him to let go, and still he would not.

One night, when his breathing was especially slow and labored, we gathered around his bed yet again to say our goodbyes. Was this the third time or the fourth? I had lost track. Once again, we started the ritual of reading and praying.

But this time was different. After a few minutes of reading, my sister called out, "Wait—I think he is moving. Maybe he is trying to tell us something!"

I glanced up from my reading and noticed slight movement under the blanket. I moved the soft blanket aside to free his large, unmistakable hands with their curved fingers. Slowly, he began to lift his hand to his face and then, with what must have taken great effort, he curled his three fingers into his thumb, lifted his pointer finger to his lips and... *SHHHHHHH.*

He shushed us! That was the end of our bedside goodbyes that night.

SINCE DAD HAD STARTED HOSPICE, none of us had slept more than two hours straight. We rotated shifts of caring for Dad and administering medications every hour, on the hour. After almost a month straight of thinking Dad was going to die "any day now," we were at our physical and emotional limits.

On August 24, 2023, we finally gave up and hired caretakers. It was clear we could no longer do it ourselves. Several hours after we called, the hospice team sent a caregiver over. They instructed us to pre-fill several syringes of morphine, lorazepam, and alprazolam so the nurse could administer them while we slept.

That night, we all went to bed and turned it over to the nurse.

33

GOODBYES AND HELLOS

A familiar song drifted through my dream, once, then twice, then three times. Eventually the song jumped out of my dream and into reality—it was my phone ringing. I grabbed for it on the floor underneath Natalie's bed, grasping for it quickly while trying not to wake her.

"Your father is in his final moments if you want to come down," an unfamiliar voice whispered.

"What? Right now?" I mumbled.

"Yes, now," the nurse responded.

I crawled out of bed and down the stairs to his room—my room. The one that used to be my office and was now full of hospital equipment and unfamiliar smells.

I grabbed his hand. "I am here Dad, I am here. I love you."

There was nothing.

"Is he... is he already gone? Did I miss it?" I croaked as I looked toward the nurse with pleading eyes.

"I'm sorry, it was very fast..."

Oh, Dad...

I wiped the hair away from his eyes—that hair. As he got thinner and his hair wilder, he started to call himself Christopher Lloyd. But at that moment, it wasn't his hair that I noticed, but his teeth. As his mouth hung slightly agape, his perfectly straight white teeth shone back at me, in sharp contrast to his severely jaundiced skin. How had I never noticed that he had such nice teeth? I couldn't look away from these perfectly white bones shining back from the hollows of his sunken face.

"He just took a few gasps—it was very fast," the nurse repeated. The poor woman was one hour away from ending her shift.

I was listening to her, but not really processing. I immediately grabbed my phone and called Launa, who answered right away.

"He's gone," I choked. "Yeah, he's gone," I repeated, followed by a sob. I made several more phone calls like that in the first few minutes. He had been hanging on for so long that I knew everyone was waiting to hear when the time had finally come.

"I know the medicine log said to give him morphine and Ativan every four hours, but at hour three he started to get really agitated," the caregiver, Monica, continued. "He started to raise his hands above his head and moan. I didn't want him to be uncomfortable, so I gave him the meds at hour three instead of four."

Vindication. Relief. Anger. I *knew* he needed more medicine than the hospice workers were telling us to give him. Their own caretaker had seen it and acted accordingly. He wasn't "stretching" —he was in pain and needed more.

But that relief was short-lived because what Monica said next haunts me to this day.

"I think he knew he was transitioning, and I think he was scared. I think he felt better after I gave him the morphine and the Ativan, because his breathing calmed, and he passed just two hours later."

I pushed the thought aside in that moment, but it is the one thing that I cannot get out of my head. Every night since his death, I think about it, and it makes me sick. I cannot bear the thought that he might have been scared in those final moments.

We waited forty minutes for the nurse to come and formally

declare him deceased. For forty minutes, I tried to make small talk with Monica while holding my dead Dad's increasingly cooling hand. I was numb, and I was scared. I had expelled so much emotion that week, so many screams/cries/tears that I was numb now, and I was afraid of how that would look to Monica and the nurse.

My whole life, Dad had defied so many odds, that when the nurse finally came a full forty minutes later, I had a fleeting thought that he might somehow still be alive. She bent down toward Dad with her stethoscope in hand, her maroon scrubs taut against her thighs. In that moment, I half-expected her to say, "I still hear a faint heartbeat." But instead, she just said, "I'm sorry" and the tears came streaming down my face, burning rivers through the familiar groves of my cheeks.

After she left, I looked at the discharge paperwork. She had checked a box, "appropriate grief observed." Appropriate. As if there's a right or wrong way to receive the news that your father is dead. But I have always been one for rule-following, and I was relieved to hear that she found my behavior "appropriate."

The nurse left, and I was left to sit alone in the room with Dad's body. By then, Mom had arrived at the house to help with the girls. It was Friday—a school day. Death does not care about schedules. I have a vague recollection of telling the girls their grandpa was gone, but I honestly don't remember much.

"I am so sorry girls; Grandpa died this morning."

"Yes, you can still wear your Rapunzel dress to school."

"No, you cannot go without underwear."

Death does not care about rules. Children do not either. My two worlds, once again colliding.

The mortuary came just thirty minutes later. They had asked if I needed more time with the body, but I did not. The body that was there on that bed was not the Dad I wanted to remember—my tall, strong, and fierce father was gone, and only a gaunt shell of him remained.

I exchanged pleasantries with the men who came and then I stepped into the kitchen while they brought in the stretcher and the bag. I sat in the kitchen, starting at the wall and trying not to imagine what those men were doing with my dad in the office. And then it came—*zzzzziiiiiiiipp*. I'm sure they tried to be quiet, but the sound of them zipping the bag over my father's face reverberated throughout the hall and into my bones. My moment of quiet solitude in the kitchen was shattered and my chest heaved as the sobs rushed out.

"We're coming around the corner," they warned, so I wouldn't have to look at the bag. My dad, in a bag. About to be discarded like trash.

I put my head down on the cool countertop and sobbed until I heard the quiet click of the door lock announcing their departure.

Suddenly, I felt an intense desire to see him off. To make sure that they were handling him correctly and taking him to the right place. I rushed into the playroom and Rob grabbed hold of me. There we stood, amongst the discarded children's toys, the wrinkled princess dresses, and broken pieces of plastic and watched through the front window as they lifted the bag, my father, into the back of the...

"Is that... a minivan?" I exclaimed.

Together, Rob and I burst into laughter at the shock of seeing the mortuary minivan.

Dad never was conventional.

———

THE LAUGHTER WAS SHORT-LIVED. With each moment that passed after Dad was gone, my anxiety grew. I became increasingly agitated and felt trapped in my house. For the last three weeks, we had been inside my house, on a hamster wheel of caretaking—administering medicine, changing bed sheets, talking to doctors, praying for Dad. And just like that, it was over. Gone. Done. No more medicine to give. No more schedules to follow.

No more.

No more.

No more.

I had to get out.

"I'm taking Dad's car and going to Zuma. I'll be home before the kids get back from school." It was the last place I had hiked with Dad, and I suddenly felt an intense urge to be there again.

Rob was smart enough not to try to discourage me.

"Be safe," he said. Then, as I was walking out the door he called out, "Hey, if you see Anthony Kiedis today, you can have a free pass!"

"Lucky for you, they're still on their world tour!" I quipped as I jumped into the car.

As I headed toward the freeway, I used Siri to send a message to Anita.

"Thank you for being here this week, exclamation point. I want you to know that I told my dad this week that I was so happy he found you, and that I could tell you loved each other, period."

How funny to be dictating such an important message to an iPhone robot, I thought.

Anita responded right away.

"It means a lot to me knowing you said that to him. I am heading to Zuma Beach and then Carpinteria; he really liked those spots."

"Wait, like... right now? I am driving to Zuma right now also," I quickly fired back, in shock.

After a few minutes of back-and-forth, we realized I was only about ten minutes behind her on the freeway and we'd be able to meet at the rock. Thank God I reached out to her beforehand. I was driving my dad's car, and she likely would have had a heart attack if she saw his car in the parking lot just hours after he died.

I had run to Zuma Rock to get away, to escape from my house. I didn't intend to do it with anybody else. My coping mechanism has always been to isolate. When I am sad or angry or upset, I curl inwards to process. The old me would have just told Anita to "go ahead" and not wait for me. But, the last three weeks had inextricably bound us together in our grief and our experiences, and sharing that together was unexpectedly comforting.

We arrived at the beach together and hugged before we started to walk through the parking lot. I wondered about the stories of all the other beach-goers. Who were all these other people at the beach at midday on a Friday? Did they not have to work? Were they there for the sun or for their souls?

I followed Anita up the hill. When she veered to the left away from the rock, I kept my mouth shut. I assumed she was taking me to some other secret place that Dad had shown her, but not me. Another hidden spot; another part of Dad I did not know.

"I guess the rock is just right around the corner, a little bit further?" Anita muttered.

Oh. She was not taking me to a secret place—she was lost.

"We actually passed the rock a while ago," I politely corrected her.

"I always just followed your dad and trusted he knew where he was going."

Well, that makes two of us, I thought.

She laughed, and we turned around together to head back to the rock.

A few minutes later, we were there. The view was stunning—cerulean water punctuated by white caps of foam as a school of dolphins revealed themselves. On such a gorgeous day, there was no reason we should have had the rock to ourselves. And yet, somehow, we were alone to sit and share our memories of Dad just hours after he had passed. We talked, we laughed, but we did not cry. It was all still too raw, too new—the loss had not yet sunk in.

Eventually, I pulled myself away, because I knew I had to get back to the house to get my kids. Anita decided to stay, and so I made the trek back to the car myself.

Point Dume is the geographical location of Zuma Rock, a place where explorers came in the 1700s. The historical marker atop the hill notes that it is "the western terminus of the Santa Monica Bay and has been an important landmark for navigators since George Vancouver's voyage in 1793."

Aside from its historical significance, most people know Point Dume as a place of great wealth, where celebrities live the California dream on this cliff atop the picturesque beaches. As I was leaving Zuma Rock, I walked toward the neighborhoods, drawn by the mystery of the massive houses and their wealthy occupants. But as I got closer to the neighborhood, I changed my mind. It felt strange—exploitative—to go there. And so, I tucked my curiosity aside and headed back to my car.

As I was leaving the parking lot, I was deep in thought, thinking of the chance encounter with Anita and how special it was to see her on that day, at that moment.

Out of the corner of my eye, I noticed a bicyclist approaching my car. A man in a fitted T-shirt and black shorts sat atop the bike. Muscular men riding bikes are a dime a dozen in Malibu. But as he rode closer, the sharp angles of his face punctuated by the black mustache came into focus, and I almost crashed my car.

Anthony. Fucking. Kiedis.

He rode past and I froze. I stopped the car and thought of what to do.

I knew that he was riding toward a dead end. There was no way he could ride his bike up the path to the rock—he would have to turn around eventually.

I made a split-second decision to back my dad's car up and pull back into the parking spot I had just left. I got out of the car and started to walk back toward the dead end. I didn't have a plan—I just needed to know it was really him. Although let's be honest, there was no way I was mistaken about that face.

A few minutes later, he came cycling back toward me. He looked so serene and nonchalant. I did a quick visual of his arms and noticed his distinct tattoos peeking out of his shirt, muscles gently flexed as he guided the bike with one hand.

I have never been obsessed with celebrities. I didn't have a favorite band growing up, or a favorite singer. I didn't have posters of N'Sync or Backstreet Boys adorning my walls as a teen. But this? This was different. In July 2022, this man had brought a light into my otherwise drab world. The Unlimited Love tour had lit a fire in me that I didn't know existed. Their music, his voice, their presence —it catapulted me into another universe. When Dad's health was declining and the kids were whining and I was at my wit's end, the one thing that could speak to my soul was the Red Hot Chili Peppers.

It's hard to fully explain to anybody what this moment meant to me. To see this musician just a few feet away from me, on the day of my dad's death, in the last place where I had hiked with my dad, was surreal.

I wanted to stop him and tell him that my dad died that day, and that his music had helped keep me afloat the past two years. But I also had so much respect for him (and let's be honest, myself) that I didn't want to throw myself at him like an obnoxious fan. So, I stayed in my lane. I stopped walking and just looked at him.

In that moment, in that space, we coexisted—me and this rockstar, together on a beach in Malibu. We looked at each other and smiled. And it was enough.

3 4

STOPPING TO FEEL

I sat atop Zuma Rock, in a different spot, on a different day. I looked down at the hidden cove, where waves crashed angrily on the shore—rocks just barely hidden from view. On one side of Zuma Rock, beachgoers lay in pristine sand, watching pelicans dive and dolphins jump. But not here. No one dared lay on this side today. Foamy water pummeled the shore and stripped away the earth, leaving the shore (what's left of it) bare and vulnerable. Not time to recover before another wave hits, shuffling everything yet again.

Rocks tumbled under the waves. The once-beautiful waters turned brown as violent waves churned up everything from below. Pelicans dared not dive here—the waves would smash them into the rocks, their limp carcasses left to float out to sea as shark bait.

And yet, amidst the foamy water there was a small pool of blindingly blue water, protected by large rocks creating a sea wall. Blue like Dad's eyes—the ones people always commented on—beautiful, but haunting. When he was mad, those eyes bore through you like lasers cutting through metal, sparks flying.

Dad was like the ocean—beautiful, turbulent, unpredictable.

Rising and falling, churning and throwing. If you know where to swim, you're safe. But venture out of calm waters, and you're bound to be mercilessly crushed by the forceful and unpredictable tide.

AFTER DAD DIED, I took a month off from work. I spent that month notifying people about his death, writing the obituary, and planning his funeral. I felt guilty being away from work, so although I wasn't talking to clients, I was still checking my email and communicating with my co-workers daily. I was trying to keep all the balls in the air.

I went back to work in September. I tried to lean into my work to avoid my deep feelings, as I had always done in the past. Work was my safe haven, where I could exist and feel successful and not have to deal with emotions. Except—it didn't work this time. I could not focus; I could not think. I would stare at the computer screen, words swimming across it meaninglessly. Suddenly, my safe place was no longer safe. I was no longer able to escape the feelings at work. I was useless everywhere.

One day, while attempting to push through, I received a phone call from a fellow lawyer. "Hey, I have a new case for you. By the way, sorry your dad died. These things happen to us at this age. I heard you took a month off, so you should be over it now, huh? So, about the case..." He droned on, but I wasn't listening.

These things happen to us at this age?

No, I screamed inside, *they don't! I am not "at that age" where we lose our parents. I am only thirty-five. Dad was only sixty-five, and he was so fit and strong! We were supposed to have at least two more decades together.*

But the part that struck me the hardest was when he said I "should be over it by now." As if losing a parent is something you just "get over." No, no, no. I was not over it. I was not even close to being over it.

I hung up the phone and sobbed in my office. I couldn't do this. I couldn't be here, pretending to be normal. I couldn't take these small condolences and move on to discussing cases. I couldn't keep going like Dad had always done—I needed to stop.

And so, I decided to take more time off work—three months, to be exact. That next week, I sat in a meeting with all my partners, while one of them shared with the others that I was experiencing an extremely high level of burn-out and that I would be taking time off to heal. Tears streamed down my face in the middle of that brand-new conference room, the one I had so carefully helped furnish just a year prior. The light streamed in through the large windows. I felt so exposed. Having all my feelings laid bare on that bright white conference room table, amongst my business partners.

But somewhere deep down, I knew—I wasn't weak. I was doing the strongest thing I had ever done: being vulnerable.

I COULDN'T COUNT how many times over the last few years that I had said, "I cannot do this anymore. I do not want my dad to die, but I just want this roller coaster to be over."

Living our lives scan to scan, chemo treatment to chemo treatment—it was too much to bear. And yet, I did. The past few years had been brutal. Always living in a constant state of unrest, waiting for the other shoe to drop. Waiting for every scan to be "the one," and then feeling secretly upset when it wasn't. Not because I wanted my dad to die—but because I couldn't live forever in that constant state of unrest.

Usually, when people go through treatment, there is a plan, a trajectory, a course of action. Dad made his own plans. He went on and off chemo whenever he felt like it. It infuriated me. Who just decides to "take a break" from chemo for six months when they are fighting an aggressive cancer? Dad, that's who. Each time he took a break, I seethed. Because I knew that it would just be a matter of time before he got another scan that said the cancer was growing, and then he would go back on the chemo. I didn't understand why he took these breaks—why not fight it with everything you've got? Stay the course? Follow a fucking plan, Dad! But, in hindsight, he was following the plan—it was just his own plan, not mine. He trusted his body and let that guide him. He knew when to push himself and when to back off, and that allowed him to live his life for the last few years on his own terms, just like he always had.

I always knew that he was terminal, and I never had the delusion that he was going to beat the cancer. I had suffered so much while his health was up and down the last few years. I wanted it to end; I wanted to return to "normal."

I thought I would feel relief when he died, knowing the battle was over, that all the ups and downs were done.

But I was wrong.

A few weeks after Dad died, I sat in Roxanne's office on a Thursday evening—our first in-person meeting in four years. I sobbed and told her, "I just didn't expect to feel this sad. Where is the relief? I thought I already grieved!"

She looked at me with her kind eyes, titled her head ever so slightly and said, "I'm sorry, Sasha. We don't get to prepay on grief."

And it hit me. I was anxious, sad and upset all those years, but I wasn't *grieving*. Dad drove me insane, made me angry, and totally confused me many times. But as difficult as he could be—he was still there. I knew that I could just text him or call him at any time. I may not have known where he was, or what he was doing, but he was *there*, somewhere.

The hardest part about grief is the stark realization that I will never see him again in this lifetime. I will never get another text from him with the "cool" emoji. I will never climb another mountain with him, or share another story about my children with him. He is gone, and I don't even know how to process that. For someone who deals with death every single day as her career, I feel shockingly unprepared for the emotional pain. He. Is. Gone.

I believe that his spirit lives on, but it's not the same as the physical presence. At one group therapy session, someone pointed out that a dragonfly was hanging around our meeting. Was that him? Is he in the trees? The oceans? The hills? Maybe. But he's not HERE. And it's so hard to explain, because our relationship was not one of emotional confidences. I don't "long for his embrace" or "yearn to hear his wisdom." I just miss his presence. His being *here*. Him. I miss him, and as naïve as it sounds, I didn't expect that. I didn't expect it to hurt so much.

When he was here, I was confused and upset. He was fighting cancer and beating the odds, and yet he was up in Washington. He wasn't using that extra time to spend every second with his kids and grandkids before he died. He was doing his own thing. I didn't understand why God was giving him this extra time, if he wasn't going to use it to be with his family? To atone for his sins. To make amends. To apologize. To be vulnerable.

When I was younger, I thought God had abandoned me in my time of need. I didn't know how any loving God could allow those things to happen to me.

But now, I realize, God hadn't abandoned me, he had guided me. And in these last few years, God wasn't giving the extra time to my dad—he was giving the extra time to *me*. For me to come to terms with who my father was, and how I could love him no matter what.

The irony is that since we got the extra time—it hurts that much more that he is gone.

Sometimes the pain is unbearable. Like a scream just constantly sitting right below the surface, about to bubble up at any second. The ironic thing is that a few times I *have* screamed, and it didn't do a damn thing to ease the ache. The invisible scream was still there, even when the real scream was coming out. I realized that I couldn't excise this grief demon with some Red Hot Chili Peppers and a few good screams. He is here to stay, for now.

35

THE CREEPY MAN

I am afraid. I have been restless at night, unable to sleep. I have started to fear the dark like a child again—worried about bad guys behind every corner of my house. The world feels less safe without him here. I didn't realize until Dad was gone how much of my sense of safety and security was tied up in his physical existence on this earth.

I knew in my bones that if something were ever to happen to me, my dad would hunt down the person who hurt me and kill them with his own bare hands. He would do everything in his power—legal or not—to protect me and my family.

But now? What now?

Logically, I know that if somebody broke into my house while Dad was living in Washington, there's not anything he could have done in the moment to protect me and my family in California. But he would be there the second I called him. He would tell me what to do, who to call, who to speak to. He knew what to do, and just the knowledge of that was hiding somewhere deep in my lizard brain for all these years.

And now, I am afraid. I feel paranoid. I am unsettled. I am unmoored.

I have started to panic about whether it was a bad idea for us to publicly post his obituary. Are some old parolees empowered now, knowing he is gone? Did he ruin someone's life at some point by sending them to prison and now they are going to come and seek revenge on us? On the one hand, I realize that I sound unhinged. On the other hand...

Where are all those people he supervised? Are they still in prison? Are they wandering the streets looking for him? It has been so long since he was working that the likelihood of them coming after him now is slim, but it's not zero.

This is something I did not expect. I did not anticipate the fear. It is not welcome, and yet, it is here. The little girl inside of me is cowering in shadows and fearing the boogeyman and I have no dad here to protect me.

SEPTEMBER 1997—I started sixth grade at Anacapa Middle School. The school was nearly triple the size of my elementary school, in both physical size and student population. The green and maroon paint peeled off the façade of the building, barely making the hulking hallways more palatable to a timid sixth-grader. The campus felt huge, vast, and scary. Thankfully, though the new school itself was a huge adjustment, I had a solid group of friends who came with me from elementary school.

One day after school, my friends and I trekked across the long sidewalk toward the YMCA parking lot. The YMCA was not affiliated with the middle school, but its parking lot abutted the school tennis courts. Savvy carpool moms had figured out that the YMCA was the best spot to facilitate pick-up and avoid the long line of cars waiting behind buses in the school parking lot.

Catherine, Julia, and I walked on the sidewalk along Telegraph Road, heading toward the YMCA parking lot. We chatted as we walked—discussing the latest Backstreet Boys song and whether N'Sync or BSB was better. We were young girls barely adjusting to our new lives as middle schoolers—teetering on the edge between children and preteens—desperately wanting to feel grown-up. And yet, the world still seemed big, threatening, and scary.

As we walked and chatted, we noticed a small sedan driving very slowly behind us. At first, it seemed like the car was slowing down to enter the YMCA parking lot. However, when I turned to look, I noticed no other cars in front of the sedan. There was no real explanation for why he was driving so slowly next to us. In fact, it almost seemed like the man was following us.

We picked up the pace and headed to the parking lot. We arrived and quickly jumped into Julia's mom's car and the three of us started talking all at once.

"A creepy man..."

"Following us in his car!"

"Yes, we are sure!"

"OMG THERE HE IS!"

Julia's mom's head turned sharply to look toward where we were all pointing. Sure enough, "the creepy man" sat in the car, staring right at us. Maybe we had been mistaken and it was a harmless misunderstanding? Surely, a stalker wouldn't be this brazen in real life, right?

Julia's mom, Cindy, rolled her window down, her arm quickly working in circles to move the window manually. She told the creepy man to "buzz off" in no uncertain terms and then we drove away.

As we drove down Telegraph Road, Cindy started to ask us about our day—what things we had learned in Algebra, and what we were reading in English. But we were too hyped-up about what had just happened to focus on boring things like our studies.

Five minutes later, Cindy was waiting at the intersection of Telegraph and Wake Forest, waiting to turn left up the street to my house. The *click-click-click-click* of the turn signal echoed loudly throughout the car. As the light turned green, the car gently accelerated and moved peacefully up the street toward my house.

We were just a few houses away from home when I turned around and looked out the back window. And there he was—the creepy man from the school idled in his sedan right behind our car.

I screamed, "HE'S STILL FOLLOWING US!"

I saw a flash of panic in Cindy's eyes as she glanced into the rearview mirror and confirmed what I had just announced. The creepy man was, in fact, behind us. She pushed on the gas and accelerated up the street toward my house. We practically blew through the stop sign before parking in front of my house. Once we parked, the man had no qualms about parking right behind us. He took out a pen and notepad and began to write.

I jumped out of the car and ran into the house. I needed to find Dad—he would know how to handle the creepy man. He was a parole officer, after all.

As suspected, Dad jumped up from his chair and ran out of the garage after I told him what had happened. He wanted to see with his own eyes. But it was too late. Cindy had already left—the creepy man close behind her.

I learned later that the creepy man followed Cindy for ten more minutes. Cindy, not wanting to drop anyone else off, drove up and down random streets, making unexpected U-turns to throw him off track. Finally, he gave up and drove away.

Three weeks later, my friends and I were walking along the same sidewalk toward the YMCA. School had just let out for the day, and we were talking with some other friends about the new cinnamon Altoid breath mints, and which of us could handle the spiciness.

As I reached into the tiny metal tin of Altoids, Catherine suddenly shrieked, "IT'S THE CREEPY MAN AGAIN!"

Sure enough, the same man sat in his old sedan, right along the sidewalk next to us. The metal tin Altoid container pinged as it hit the sidewalk, breath mints rolling every which way as we began to run like our lives depended on it. We ran to Cindy's car that was once again waiting—unsuspectingly—in the YMCA lot.

This time, the man wasn't dumb enough to pull into the lot behind us. This time, he sped off.

We raced back to my house and once again I couldn't wait to get out of the car to tell Dad what had happened. This time, Cindy came inside to corroborate my story. "Do you think we should report this to the police?" she inquired. "Do you know somebody that could help us?"

"Of course I do. My buddy is the watch commander down at Ventura Police Department. I will give him a call."

The next day, Dad drove me down to the police station to make a report. He told me that all I needed to do was tell the police what had happened. There was nothing to fear. I was calm when I spoke to the police officer. I watched as he jotted down notes and nodded his head slowly while I was talking. I wasn't intimidated by the small, carpeted room or the gun on the officer's waist. I felt safe because Dad was with me. I knew that nothing bad would happen to me or my friends, because Dad was in our corner.

After that day, we never saw the creepy man again.

In later years, I jokingly referred to this as the "stalker incident." I would tell new friends about how I had a stalker in middle school. But I downplayed it as no big deal—just a weird dude who followed me home one day. *He was probably just bored, and it wasn't a real threat,* I told myself. *You know how young kids exaggerate.*

DECEMBER 2023—I sat on the floor in a hotel room in Blaine, Washington, my legs splayed out at my side. My children watched

Lorax at top volume, and I tried not to panic about the mounds of Dad's personal stuff that surrounded me.

We had come up for a final weekend visit to Washington to clean out Dad's house before selling it. I was terrified of shipping Dad's things—afraid to lose them in transit—and so I had brought as much as possible back to that hotel room to stuff into our suitcases.

It was there, amongst the piles of personal property and Dad's paperwork, that I stumbled upon a picture of the creepy man. And not just any picture, but the booking photograph for Mr. Francis Gerard. Age twenty-five. Convicted of stalking and attempted molestation of a child under age fourteen.

I physically recoiled and a small gasp caught in my throat. The creepy man was no joke. I never realized how much danger I was in at that time. Dad kept me safe—from the creepy man, and from the seriousness of the danger that I had been in. But Dad never forgot. Decades later, he was still tracking Mr. Gerard's whereabouts and making sure that I was safe.

36

GENERATIONAL WEALTH

Taking time off work was terrifying. There was nothing left to distract me from my feelings and from the pain I felt after losing Dad. It took my breath away daily. For as much as he drove me crazy, I loved him. He was part of me; he was part of the fiber of my being. I know now why Dad never stopped moving, why he always kept going—because the pain you feel when you really sit with your grief and just *feel* it, is so immense it is suffocating.

In those three months off work, I stopped to feel. And the feelings were so overwhelming, so powerful, they took on a mind of their own. But I needed to do something different than Dad had done. I needed to force myself to feel the grief and pain. I saw how stuffing his feelings for decades had wreaked havoc on my father. Those times he was angry and demanding weren't because he was a bad person; he was a person fighting to maintain control. Maintaining a semblance of control was the only way he knew how to cope with the enormous losses he had experienced. The neglect and abuse he suffered as a child, the losses of five of his siblings, the violence he witnessed at work, the divorce and the splitting up of our family, the cancer.

He couldn't bear to deal with those feelings because he had no tools for how to be vulnerable, for how to admit pain and sadness and grief. And so, he drank, and he exercised, and he controlled, because that's all he knew how to do.

But I couldn't do that to myself. I had been trying for too long, but I needed to break the cycle. I needed to admit the pain and lay myself bare for others to see. I needed others to know that we can feel immense grief and sadness, and still survive.

After Dad died, I spent many afternoons hiking alone and thinking of him. One day, I hiked through Sycamore Canyon, the place where Dad had taken us on that epic bike ride as children. I thought of him running down the hill, looking back at me, urging me to keep going so that I wouldn't crash. "Just keep peddling!" he had yelled at me over his shoulder.

That day, I tried to push myself to hike higher and higher up the mountain, to reach the peak. But I was tired, and I was sad. I missed Dad. Tears burned behind my eyes as I looked forward and saw I still had half a mile to go to the top.

But I didn't need to keep going. I didn't need to push through the pain this time. It was okay to stop. It was okay to feel. It was okay to scream and to weep and to show that pain to others.

And so, I stopped.

I turned around.

I went home to my husband and my young daughters. I allowed them to see my raw grief, to see my tears and to wrap me in their arms and tell me I was going to be okay.

Because allowing myself to let my walls down and be vulnerable in front of those I love is the true gift of generational wealth Dad left me.

EPILOGUE

I sat at my office desk, staring at the computer screen. *Zoom has notified the host that you joined. Host will let you in soon.* A lump formed in my throat as I saw those words and the bright blue Zoom logo.

A few minutes later, my host joined the virtual room. Her chestnut hair fell loosely over her shoulders, and her deep brown eyes stared back at me with a comforting gentleness.

"Hello, Sasha," she started in a soothing voice. "Welcome."

"Hi," I responded, and then I started rambling. "I have no idea what I am doing. I have never done anything like this before. To be honest, I didn't, um, really believe in all this before... honestly, I am not sure if I even do believe in it now. Do you ask me questions? Do I ask you questions? What do I do?"

The woman held up a yellow pad of paper—a legal pad, a familiar sight to all lawyers. I instantly felt a connection and as I exhaled, my shoulders released a bit of the tension they had been holding. Funny how a piece of paper can have such an impact.

"It's okay," she said. "You don't have to do anything but listen. I already have all these notes to share with you." As she responded, she turned the yellow pad toward the screen. Though I couldn't make out any of the words, it was clear that the page was full, from top to bottom, with handwritten notes.

And then she began. She explained to me that she has a connection to other realms that enable her to see, hear, and communicate with spirit guides.

She then explained that she could very clearly see a tall, handsome man in a field of flowers, and that he was telling her he was free from pain.

I instantly started crying. Wherever he was, he was free.

"Your father wants you to know that he is at peace, more so than he ever was in life. He knows that he made it hard for you in the end, and he is sorry. He fought the cancer as hard as he could, and he knows that made it harder for you and your sister. He is so sorry..."

The tears poured down my face, but I didn't bother to stop them as they passed my cheeks and dripped off my chin.

"He knows he wasn't gracious in the end—he was angry. He wasn't ready to go. He didn't think it was his time, and he wasn't ready. But he's at peace with it now, and he wants you to be at peace with it, too."

To my left, a candle flickered. I pulled the blanket on my lap closer to my chest as I curled my feet up onto my chair and continued to listen.

"He is telling me that he's sorry you had to see him like that—so unhappy and not ready to go. He was panicking and trying to hold on as tight as possible because he was losing control. He's sorry that he was so psychologically weak..."

In life, the closest I ever got to an apology from Dad was the "Coo Coo for Coco Puffs" comment in Lake Tahoe. Dad never so much as gave a hint that he had any remorse for any of his behaviors.

But here he was, telling me repeatedly how sorry he was. In death, he could be far more honest than he ever could in life. I didn't realize just how much I needed to hear those words: "I'm sorry." I needed the acknowledgement to prove what I had always suspected —that underneath his rock-hard exterior was a scared young boy who needed someone to comfort him. Now he was finally capable of seeing that no matter how much he loved me, no matter how often he told me he was proud of me, sometimes he also hurt me.

I had scheduled the appointment with the Medium out of desperation, really. I didn't expect it to be legitimate. I thought people like her gave broad, generic information that grieving people would mold to fit their stories—desperate to make something out of nothing.

But I was wrong.

For the next hour, the Medium continued to share bits of information with me that shook me to my core. She shared things she heard from my dad that nobody but me would have known— things that happened in the last hours of his life, in the intimacy of my home. Things I didn't share with friends, or family, and especially not social media. And yet, she knew. Because he knew.

He is out there, somewhere, and he is at peace.

For months after his death, I was haunted by the fact that he was scared to die. I was haunted by the fear that I had killed him by starting the hospice too soon. Intellectually, I knew that he had terminal cancer. I knew that he had stopped eating. I knew that he was in excruciating pain and that the regular medications were no longer working. And yet, I still couldn't shake my emotional anguish over the fear that I had killed him. I couldn't stop thinking that if we had done something different, he could have lasted longer. Despite everything that my eyes had seen, my heart still told me that I had killed him.

And in this one-hour Zoom meeting, this stranger put all those fears to bed once and for all. It wasn't my fault. The cancer killed him—not me.

After an hour, we began to wind down the session. Before we concluded, she relayed the following image:

"Your father is standing in a field of flowers holding a book. No, not just holding it, but waving it around. That's curious," she began quizzically. "I wonder what he is doing with that book?"

My heart sped up.

"Oh wait, he's talking again... He is telling me, 'She's a great writer. I am so proud of her. Her book—she will finish it and it will heal her. Her book will be better than mine ever was.'"

By the time I met with the Medium, I had been secretly working on this book for months. Nobody knew except Rob.

The Medium tilted her head to the side and looked at me enquiringly. "I'm sorry, this seems different from everything else he has been telling me today. Does this book comment make sense to you?"

With that, I just smiled, as silent tears of joy streamed down my face.

REVIEW REQUEST

Dear Reader,

Writing this memoir was the most vulnerable thing I have ever done. But it was also the most healing thing I have ever done. If *Stopping to Feel* made you feel safe to share your *own* stories, I'd love to hear about it. If you feel empowered by this memoir, please contact me directly through social media @author_slcollins.

Also, if you enjoyed *Stopping to Feel*, I'd really appreciate it if you could take a couple minutes to write a review on Storygraph, Amazon, or Goodreads—even a single sentence will do! Please also share it on your own social media. These reviews make a surprisingly huge difference in the impact of a book.

Many thanks,

S.L. Collins

ACKNOWLEDGMENTS

To my husband, Rob. Thank you for not running for the hills after my dad challenged you to a stick fight at age nineteen. Through all the ups and downs, you have been my most constant. Thank you for choosing me, every single day. I love you and I will always be your Creature.

To my daughters, Nadia and Natalie. Just because motherhood isn't always easy for me doesn't mean it isn't worth it. Thank you for reminding me not to take myself so seriously, and for loving me unconditionally, even when I make you clean up your toys and brush your teeth. I love you both to pieces.

To my sister, Launa, without whom I would never have survived the stories that make up this book. Thank you for getting it. Thank you for being willing to have hard conversations. You make me a better person and I am forever grateful to have you in my life. I love you.

To my brother-in-law, James. Thank you for all the times you packed up that minivan and drove your whole family up here to help support Dad. And thank you for washing the dog...

To my nephew, Nipsey. Thanks for bringing joy into a very hard year. You're the cutest.

To my mom, Kelly. Thank you for encouraging me to share my memories, even when they weren't always the easiest to relive. Thanks for making my childhood as normal as possible, even when shit hit the fan. I love you and am so proud of all the work we have done to heal and change the trajectory of our family.

To my stepdad, Tom. I hope Tommy and Dad are somewhere

beautiful. Thank you for loving my kids as your own and helping us create new memories. I promise we will make the soccer sign ups next year.

To my mother-in-law, Debbie. Thank you for all the love you heaped on the girls over the last several years when I was in my lowest points. I am so grateful for you.

To my sister-in-law, Bree. Thank you for being an ear to Rob when I was emotionally checked out and thanks for being the best Tia B to our girls.

To my beta readers, Natasha, Sarah, and Jacquelyn. I am forever indebted to you for your opinions, critiques, and encouragements. Thank you for helping me take something rough and polish it.

To my Thriving Author's Academy pod sisters, there is absolutely no way that I would have been able to do this without your weekly support. I miss our Thursday nights.

To my Elephants. I hope you know who you are. Thank you for welcoming me to your herd six years ago and for lifting me when I was down. Thank you for loving me and supporting me, unconditionally. I would be lost without you.

To Dallas Woodburn, my book doula. I am forever grateful to the universe for bringing us back together after all these years. I knew you were going to big places ever since you wrote *There's A Huge Pimple On My Nose* in fifth grade. I never imagined I'd be standing here with you. Thank you for your unrelenting support and encouragement.

And last, but not least, to Dad. I hope you're still proud of me. I love you and I miss you.

ABOUT THE AUTHOR

S.L. Collins is a partner at a law firm where she practices in the area of trusts and estates. All of her awards are related to her career, and while she's very proud of them, she is also trying to become a person who is not focused solely on professional achievements. She is a woman who has recently accepted that she has no control over anything but her own attitudes and reactions, and that has given her abundant peace and serenity. She lives in Southern California with her husband, two daughters, and two adorable dogs who drive her crazy.